HIGH NOON Spelling
LEVEL C

JENNIFER ASHLOCK

High Noon Books
Novato, California

Available from High Noon Books

High Noon Spelling Program

Level A   ISBN 1-57128-304-8
Level B   ISBN 1-57128-305-6
Level C   ISBN 1-57128-350-1
Level D   ISBN 1-57128-351-X

Cover design: Jill Zwicky
Interior design: Lucy Nielson and Bonni Gatter

Copyright © 2004 by High Noon Books. All rights reserved. Printed in the United States of America. No part of this publication may be reproduced, stored in a retrieval system, or transmitted, in any form or by any means, electronic, mechanical photocopying, or otherwise, without the prior written permission of the publisher, unless otherwise indicated.

High Noon Books

A division of Academic Therapy Publications
20 Commercial Boulevard
Novato, CA 94949-7249

800-422-7249

International Standard Book Number 1-57128-350-1

Order #8350-1

Table of Contents

Program Description 4

Using This Program 5
   Determining student entry point 5
   Weekly schedule 5

Using the Lessons 6
   Core Activities 6
   Independent Activities 6

Lesson 1	Review: Initial & final digraphs: *sh, wh, th*	8
Lesson 2	Review: Initial and final *ch*, final *tch*, initial *ph*, initial *thr*	12
Lesson 3	Review: Initial *wr*, initial *kn*, final *mb*	16
Lesson 4	Review: /or/ spelled *or, ore, oar*	20
Lesson 5	Review:/er/ spelled *er, ir, ur*	24
Lesson 6	Review: /oo/ as in *look* and *hoot*; /aw/ spelled *aw, au*	28
Lesson 7	Inflectional endings: *-s, -es*; (irregular dropped *–e*)	32
Lesson 8	Inflectional endings: *ed* (dropped *–e*)	36
Lesson 9	Inflectional endings: *ed* (dropped *–e*, doubling)	40
Lesson 10	Inflectional endings: *–ng* (dropped *–e*)	44
Lesson 11	Final digraphs: *sh, ch*	48
Lesson 12	Review: Inflectional endings: *-s, -es, ed, ing* (dropped *–e*, doubling)	52
Lesson 13	Word endings: *y*	56
Lesson 14	Inflectional endings: *–ies, –ied*	60
Lesson 15	Comparatives: *er, est*	64
Lesson 16	Comparatives: *-iest, -ier*	68
Lesson 17	Introduction to syllables: compound words	72
Lesson 18	Review: Comparatives	76
Lesson 19	Prefixes: *dis-, un-*	80
Lesson 20	Prefixes: *re-, un-*	84
Lesson 21	Suffixes: *-ful, -ly*	88
Lesson 22	Suffixes: *–less, –ress*	92
Lesson 23	Syllable rules: VCCV (double and different - schwa)	96
Lesson 24	Review: Prefixes and Suffixes: *dis-, un-, re-*	100
Lesson 25	Syllable rules: VCCV and VCV long (schwa)	104
Lesson 26	Syllable rules: VCV short and VCV long (schwa)	108
Lesson 27	Syllable rules: silent *–e* (schwa)	112
Lesson 28	Syllable rules: with r-controlled (*er, or*)	116
Lesson 29	Syllable rules with prefixes (*re, un, dis* – schwa)	120
Lesson 30	Review: Syllable rules	124
Lesson 31	Prefixes: *im-, in-*	128
Lesson 32	Prefix: *mis-, pre-*	132
Lesson 33	Prefix: *pre-, de-*	136
Lesson 34	Controlled *w/l*	140
Lesson 35	Suffixes: *-er/-or*	144
Lesson 36	Review: Prefixes: *im–, in–, mis–, pre–, de–*	148

Answer Key 152

Appendix A
   Posttest 159
   Word Sort 160

Appendix B
   Stimulus Sentences 161

Appendix C
   Games 172

To the Teacher

High Noon Spelling is designed to give your students multiple opportunities for practice in spelling and writing. The ability to write the letters of words in proper phonetic sequence forms the foundation for communicating in writing as well as for decoding familiar and new words while reading. A student's familiarity with the ordered patterns and rules of the English language also supports the building and expansion of vocabulary, thus broadening the scope of all language opportunities.

Program Description

High Noon Spelling consists of four levels that each can be used as a complete one-year on-level spelling program for students in grades 2 to 5 or as a remedial spelling program for older students who need carefully sequenced spelling instruction.

Each level of *High Noon Spelling* includes 36 lessons, each with four reproducible pages:

Page 1—PRETEST Lists 18 spelling words along with space for two challenge words. Students fold the page to take the pretest and space is provided for students to write corrections.

Page 2—WORD SORT Students sort words into categories that focus their attention on phonics concepts that lead to better spelling. On this page they also read and write sight words and tricky spelling words in sentences.

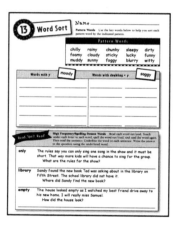

Page 3—READING, WRITING & SPELLING Here students are offered a variety of related activities. Students proofread words, sentences, and paragraphs; write responses; and use sentence context to identify words.

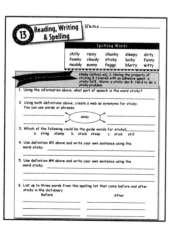

Page 4—WORD PLAY These pages offer a range of fun activities that reinforce spelling skills: word building, word search, mixed-up letters, crossword puzzles, and coding activities.

Review Lessons

Skills are reviewed every sixth lesson.

Page 1—PRETEST
The pattern words on the Review lists are new words using the same spelling patterns from the previous five lessons. Sight words have been chosen from the previous five lessons.

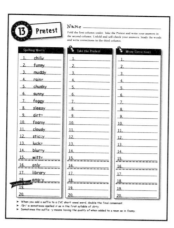

Page 2—WORD SORT
Eighteen pattern words have been included for the Review sort. To help students further internalize spelling patterns, the words chosen are taken from the pretest page and include additional pattern words.

Using this Program

Determining student entry point

For below-level small groups and individuals, use an informal assessment to place students at appropriate starting level and lesson. It may be helpful to determine an appropriate entry point for students by referring to the table of contents of this book for skills you know have not been mastered.

Weekly Schedule

Each lesson in High Noon Spelling can be taught over the course of five days.

Day 1	*Pretest* for the week
Day 2	*Word Sort* activity
Day 3	*Reading, Writing & Spelling* activity
Day 4	*Word Play* activity
Day 5	*Posttest* for the week

Lessons can be accelerated by teaching only the *Pretest*, *Word Sort*, and *Post-test* pages. Additional options for days 3 and 4 are to use the games or sort grid to repeat the sort found in Appendix A. If these are used as options, the *Reading, Writing & Spelling* or *Word Play* activities can be used as homework.

Using the Lessons

Each page in a lesson should take approximately 20 minutes to complete. The Core Activities in each lesson are the Pretest, Word Sort, and Posttest pages. These activities are essential for instruction and assessment of the skills taught in each lesson.

The *Reading, Writing & Spelling* and *Word Play* pages provide **Extra Practice Activities** that reinforce the skills taught in each lesson. These pages can also be used for homework or additional class work. Ideally students should receive some spelling instruction daily using one of many options provided.

Core Activities

1. **Taking the *Pretest***

   Read aloud the spelling words listed in the first column. You may want to add challenge words to the list that fit the same spelling patterns taught in the lesson or add important content words. Have students write these words in the lines at the bottom of the column. Refer students to the spelling rules printed at the bottom of the page.

   Ask students to fold the page so that the first column is not visible. Tell them to listen carefully and write the words they hear on the lines in the second column. Refer to the stimulus sentences for each lesson in Appendix B. Then read each word in the Spelling Words list, followed by the stimulus sentence. Then repeat the word.

   Once students have finished writing, ask them to unfold their papers. They should check their spellings against the words in the first row. Any words that are spelled incorrectly should be written in the appropriate line in the third column.

2. **Doing the *Word Sort***

   Read aloud the words listed in the Pattern Words column. Read the directions aloud with students, indicating and reading the key words positioned at the top of each sorting column. Students should then write the pattern words in the appropriate column. There is a word sort grid provided in Appendix A for students who would benefit from cutting and sorting their spelling words.

   In the *Read, Spell, Read!* portion of the page, read the directions aloud with students. Students should read each high-frequency or tricky spelling word out loud, then read it in the sentence before underlining the word. Assist students with identifying and pronouncing words in the sentence. Students then write a complete sentence response using the high frequency or tricky spelling word in the space provided.

3. **Taking the *Posttest***

   See Appendix A for the Posttest. Tell students to listen carefully and write the words they hear on the lines provided. Refer to the stimulus sentences in Appendix B. Read aloud the spelling words and challenge words listed on the Pretest page.

Independent Activities

The *Reading, Writing & Spelling* and *Word Play* pages are designed to be completed independently by students in the classroom or at home. You should work through the first of these pages with students to familiarize them with the activity types.

The lessons in *High Noon Spelling* are flexible and allow opportunities for differentiated instruction based on the needs of individual students. The following chart shows methods for providing extra support, or extra challenge, in the activity types in the *Reading, Writing & Spelling* and *Word Play* pages.

Activity type	Lesson page	Extra Support	Challenge
Writing	*Reading, Writing & Spelling*	Ask students to write sentences with selected words instead of a paragraph.	Ask students to write more than one paragraph, or challenge students to try to use all the spelling words in their writing.
Clues	*Reading, Writing & Spelling*	Read the clues to students and have them complete the page with a partner or in a small group. Build vocabulary as needed.	Ask students to write their own clues for the spelling words.
Dictionary Use	*Reading, Writing & Spelling*	Guide students through this activity, explaining the multiple meanings. Only contrast two meanings instead of three or four.	Ask students to create cartoons and write captions for all the multiple meanings of the word featured.
Proofreading Paragraphs	*Reading, Writing & Spelling*	Guide students through this activity, working together to find and correct errors.	Ask students to write the passages correctly, adding describing words and phrases.
Fill in the Blank	*Reading, Writing & Spelling*	Read the sentences to students and have them complete the page with a partner or in a small group. Build vocabulary as needed.	Ask students to create their own *Fill in the Blank* page for the weekly spelling words.
Word Paths	*Word Play*	Fill in the words for students in the far right hand column. Only ask them to connect the paths.	Ask students to create their own path puzzle page with Challenge Words or words with the same spelling pattern for the week.
Word Find	*Word Play*	Guide students through this activity, giving clues to help them find words. You may want to give this assignment to pairs of students.	Have students create their own *Word Find*.
Exploring Words	*Word Play*	Guide students through this activity, completing the page together. The blank sorting grid in Appendix A can be used to write down all the words. Have students first cut apart words, and then cut apart individual word parts.	Have students search through literature or reading materials to find words with the same word parts that are featured in this activity.
Crossword	*Word Play*	Give additional letter clues before students start the crossword.	Encourage students to create their own *Crossword* puzzles using the words from their spelling lists.
Coding	*Word Play*	Guide students through this activity, helping them find the words to crack the code.	Give students fewer words to crack the code on.

The Answer Key for all lessons is located on page 152.

Pretest

Name _____

Fold the first column under. Take the Pretest and write your answers in the second column. Unfold and self-check your answers. Study the words and write corrections in the third column.

Spelling Words	Take the Pretest	Write Corrections
1. shame	1.	1.
2. whisk	2.	2.
3. thud	3.	3.
4. brush	4.	4.
5. crush	5.	5.
6. when	6.	6.
7. wheat	7.	7.
8. math	8.	8.
9. thank	9.	9.
10. cloth	10.	10.
11. which	11.	11.
12. thing	12.	12.
13. sheet	13.	13.
14. shock	14.	14.
15. fresh	15.	15.
16. other	16.	16.
17. breath	17.	17.
18. breathe	18.	18.

Challenge Words

19.	19.	19.
20.	20.	20.

➤ /sh/ is usually spelled *sh* as in *mash*.
➤ /th/ is spelled *th* as in *thin*.
➤ /hw/ is usually spelled *wh* as in *whiz*.

# Word Sort

Name _____

Pattern Words Use the key words below to help you sort each pattern word by the indicated pattern.

Pattern Words
shame   whisk   thud   brush   crush
when   wheat   math   thank   cloth
which   thing   sheet   shock   fresh

Initial *sh* Words [show]	Final *sh* Words [smash]	Initial *th* Words [thin]	Final *th* Words [path]	Initial *wh* Words [white]

Read, Spell, Read!

High Frequency/Tricky Words Read each word out loud. Touch under each letter in each word, spell the word out loud, and read the word again. Then read the sentence. Underline the word in each sentence. Write the answer to the question using the underlined word.

other — Phil could only find one sock by his boot. He must have lost the other one at the gym.
   What did Phil find at the gym?

_____

breathe — Beth and Jay had lots of fun on their hike. Beth stopped on the trail to breathe in the fresh, clean air.
   What did Beth stop to do?

_____

breath — The race was run at a fast pace. When she was done, Kim was out of breath.
   How did Kim feel when the race was done?

_____

Copyright © 2004 by High Noon Books. Permission granted to reproduce for classroom use.

LESSON 1

Reading, Writing & Spelling

Name _____

Spelling Words

shame	whisk	thud	brush	crush	when
wheat	math	thank	cloth	which	thing
sheet	shock	fresh	breath	breathe	other

Writing

The kids in your class love the cake you brought for the party. Write down how to make the cake for your pals. Use at least five of your spelling words.

_____

_____

_____

_____

_____

_____

_____

_____

_____

_____

Check the following after you have proofread your writing.

☐ Check here if you proofread for **misspelled** words.

☐ Check here if you proofread for **words** you may have **left out** of your writing.

☐ Check here if you proofread for **punctuation.**

☐ Check here if you reread your writing to make sure it **makes sense.**

List below the spelling words from your list that you used in your writing.

_____

_____

List other words that were hard to spell. Proofread and check spellings.

_____

_____

Name _____

Word Play

Spelling Words

shame	whisk	thud	brush	crush	when
wheat	math	thank	cloth	which	thing
sheet	shock	fresh	breath	breathe	other

Word Paths — Connect one letter from each row to the next to find all the letters in one of your spelling words. Then write the word on the line provided. Each letter should be used once.

S	R	A	A	H
C	H	E	S	E
F	R	E	S	H
W	H	U	M	T

1. shame
2. _____
3. _____
4. _____

S	H	O	E	H
W	T	E	E	R
O	H	H	C	K
S	H	I	C	T

5. _____
6. _____
7. _____
8. _____

T	H	I	D	
W	H	U	S	G
T	H	T	N	
M	A	I	H	K

9. _____
10. _____
11. _____
12. _____

B	R	E	T	K
W	H	O	N	H
C	L	U	N	H
T	H	A	S	

13. _____
14. _____
15. _____
16. _____

Pretest

Name _____

Fold the first column under. Take the Pretest and write your answers in the second column. Unfold and self-check your answers. Study the words and write corrections in the third column.

Spelling Words	Take the Pretest	Write Corrections
1. chain	1.	1.
2. scratch	2.	2.
3. phone	3.	3.
4. three	4.	4.
5. speech	5.	5.
6. throne	6.	6.
7. champ	7.	7.
8. twitch	8.	8.
9. graph	9.	9.
10. switch	10.	10.
11. beach	11.	11.
12. match	12.	12.
13. cheese	13.	13.
14. throw	14.	14.
15. catch	15.	15.
16. often	16.	16.
17. enough	17.	17.
18. phase	18.	18.
Challenge Words		
19.	19.	19.
20.	20.	20.

➤ /ch/ is sometimes spelled *tch* at the end of a word or syllable after a short vowel.
➤ /ch/ is usually spelled *ch* as in *much*.
➤ /thr/ is spelled *thr* as in *thrash*.
➤ /th/ is usually spelled *th* as in *bath* or *then*.
➤ /f/ is sometimes spelled *ph* as in *phone*.

Name _____

Pattern Words Use the key words below to help you sort each pattern word by the indicated pattern.

Pattern Words

chain	champ	cheese	speech	beach	three
throne	throw	scratch	twitch	graph	switch
match	catch	phone	often	enough	phase

Initial *ch* Words [chill]	Final *tch* Words [patch]	Initial *thr* Words [threw]	Final *ch* Words [munch]	Initial *ph* Words [phase]

Read, Spell, Read!

High Frequency/Tricky Words Read each word out loud. Touch under each letter in each word, spell the word out loud, and read the word again. Then read the sentence. Underline the word in each sentence. Write the answer to the question using the underlined word.

often — Jill goes to the beach as often as she can. She likes to swim in the sea.
   When does Jill go to the beach?

enough — Rich needs to get enough snacks to feed five boys. They will be here soon to watch the game.
   What does Rich have to get?

phase — Pam's new house would be built soon! Part of the last phase of the job will be to choose the paint.
   When will Pam choose the paint?

13

Reading, Writing & Spelling

Name _____

Pattern Words

chain	champ	cheese	speech	beach	three
throne	throw	scratch	twitch	graph	switch
match	catch	phone	often	enough	phase

Clues
Read the clues. Choose the spelling word that best fits the clue.

1. It's a food made from milk. _____
2. Rabbits do this with their noses. _____
3. You can use it to start a camp fire. _____
4. It comes after two. _____
5. It means to do lots of times. _____
6. It means to change. _____
7. It means you are the one who won. _____
8. It means you don't need more. _____
9. It rhymes with *beach*. _____
10. When you itch you do this. _____
11. People talk on it. _____
12. It rhymes with *maze*. _____
13. You do this when a ball is hit. _____
14. It has links and is very strong. _____

Each group of words below represents a category. Find a spelling word that could be grouped with each category and write it on the line provided.

1. crown, king, queen, robe _____
2. sand, waves, sea, fish _____
3. pitch, fling, hurl _____

Name _____

Pattern Words

chain	champ	cheese	speech	beach	three
throne	throw	scratch	twitch	graph	switch
match	catch	phone	often	enough	phase

Word Find

Find the spelling words in the word find puzzle below. Circle each word.

M	X	Y	J	P	O	R	N	A	S	E	R	T	I	M	N	P	Q
L	A	D	C	O	E	P	H	A	S	E	A	R	H	A	O	L	P
T	T	T	S	L	I	R	P	G	E	Q	P	D	B	R	P	O	N
U	L	H	C	W	G	F	F	P	S	D	H	C	R	Q	O	O	H
S	P	F	K	H	I	N	U	T	H	R	O	W	A	I	J	N	T
P	B	S	M	N	S	T	M	E	M	P	N	T	B	O	F	H	E
A	G	S	A	B	R	I	C	A	L	T	E	N	O	U	G	H	N
T	B	U	T	H	S	S	H	H	N	X	P	X	D	C	R	S	T
C	E	W	L	O	K	T	E	K	C	A	R	B	C	H	I	P	S
H	A	C	H	A	M	P	E	P	F	O	M	U	N	C	H	E	M
M	C	H	J	F	P	E	S	U	D	O	L	O	K	T	U	E	Q
L	H	I	S	N	Y	Z	E	O	L	C	X	H	R	T	L	C	T
A	T	L	E	C	T	W	I	T	C	H	C	P	T	H	U	H	O
O	L	T	X	T	R	K	B	D	P	T	K	X	G	R	A	P	H
R	F	F	S	N	D	A	U	O	A	A	Z	E	N	E	S	P	E
O	J	E	U	B	T	R	T	C	N	P	Y	F	L	E	M	L	O
C	T	H	R	E	W	T	S	C	M	X	M	N	P	H	H	S	E
S	X	P	Q	L	P	D	L	C	H	A	I	N	P	H	R	A	T

15

Pretest

Name _____

Fold the first column under. Take the Pretest and write your answers in the second column. Unfold and self-check your answers. Study the words and write corrections in the third column.

Spelling Words	Take the Pretest	Write Corrections
1. wrong	1.	1.
2. knock	2.	2.
3. limb	3.	3.
4. gnu	4.	4.
5. thumb	5.	5.
6. knife	6.	6.
7. wreath	7.	7.
8. wrist	8.	8.
9. kneel	9.	9.
10. gnat	10.	10.
11. known	11.	11.
12. gnaw	12.	12.
13. climb	13.	13.
14. write	14.	14.
15. lamb	15.	15.
16. answer	16.	16.
17. height	17.	17.
18. ache	18.	18.

Challenge Words

| 19. | 19. | 19. |
| 20. | 20. | 20. |

➤ /n/ is sometimes spelled *kn* as in *knit* or *gn* as in *gnat*.
➤ /r/ is sometimes spelled *wr* as in *write*.
➤ /m/ is sometimes spelled *mb* at the end of a word as in *dumb*.

Word Sort

Name _____

Pattern Words Use the key words below to help you sort each pattern word by the indicated pattern.

Pattern Words				
wrong	wreath	wrist	write	knock
knife	kneel	known	gnu	gnat
gnaw	limb	thumb	climb	lamb

Initial *wr* Words — wrote	Initial *kn* Words — know	Initial *gn* Words — gnarl	Final *mb* Words — comb

Read, Spell, Read!

High Frequency/Tricky Words Read each word out loud. Touch under each letter in each word, spell the word out loud, and read the word again. Then read the sentence. Underline the word in each sentence. Write the answer to the question using the underlined word.

answer — Mrs. Brown put the answer on the board. The kids were told to check their own work.
   What did Mrs. Brown put on the board?

_____

ache — When he swam all day, Gage got an ache in his arm. Ice should help when he gets home.
   What did Gage get when he swam all day?

_____

height — Pete has grown so much since last year. His height is now five feet tall!
   How tall is Pete?

_____

17

Reading, Writing & Spelling

Name _____

Answer the following questions about your spelling words. Use the dictionary definitions below.

Spelling Words

wrong	wreath	wrist	write	knock
knife	knee	known	gnu	gnat
gnaw	limb	thumb	climb	lamb

Dictionary & Vocabulary Connections

limb (lim) *n.* **1.** One of the large branches of a tree: *The cat sat on a tree limb.* **2.** One of the jointed parts of an animal, such as an arm, leg, or wing. *The dog broke at least one limb.*

1. Using the information above, what part or parts of speech is the word *limb*?
   _____

2. Using all definitions above, create a web of synonyms for *limb*. You can use words or phrases.

   _____   limb   _____

3. Which of the following could be the guide words for *limb*? _____
   a. lime   line   b. like   line   c. link   list

4. Use definition #1 above and write your own sentence using the word *limb*.
   _____
   _____

5. Use definition #2 above and write your own sentence using the word *limb*.
   _____
   _____

6. List up to three words from the spelling list that come before and after *limb* in the dictionary.

   Before   After
   _____   _____
   _____   _____
   _____   _____

Name _____

Spelling Words

wrong	wreath	wrist	write	knock	knife
kneel	known	gnu	gnat	gnaw	limb
thumb	climb	lamb	answer	height	ache

Crossword — Use the clues provided to fill in the crossword puzzle with your spelling words. Only use each word once.

Across
2. reply to a question
3. to chew
6. a bug
8. you grab with it
9. you cut with it
11. a sound you make on a door
13. a pain
14. this is how tall you are
15. a leg or an arm

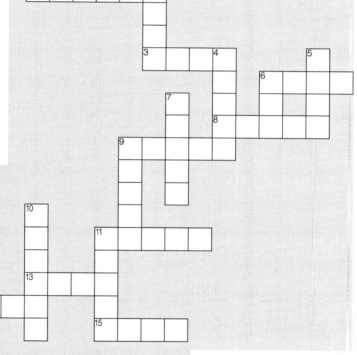

Down
1. not right
4. done with a pen
5. a young sheep
6. it has fur and legs
7. to go up
9. it is in your mind
10. it is made from a plant
11. you bend with your knees to do this
12. it is next to your arm

Copyright © 2004 by High Noon Books. Permission granted to reproduce for classroom use.

Pretest

Name _____

Fold the first column under. Take the Pretest and write your answers in the second column. Unfold and self-check your answers. Study the words and write corrections in the third column.

Spelling Words	Take the Pretest	Write Corrections
1. torch	1.	1.
2. store	2.	2.
3. oar	3.	3.
4. chore	4.	4.
5. porch	5.	5.
6. sport	6.	6.
7. soar	7.	7.
8. score	8.	8.
9. horse	9.	9.
10. shore	10.	10.
11. storm	11.	11.
12. board	12.	12.
13. tore	13.	13.
14. north	14.	14.
15. thorn	15.	15.
16. little	16.	16.
17. heard	17.	17.
18. sugar	18.	18.

Challenge Words

19.	19.	19.
20.	20.	20.

➤ /or/ is usually spelled *or* as in *cork*.
➤ /or/ is sometimes spelled *oar* or *ore* as in *soar* or *core*.

20

Copyright © 2004 by High Noon Books. Permission granted to reproduce for classroom use.

Word Sort

Name _____

Pattern Words Use the key words below to help you sort each pattern word by the indicated pattern.

Pattern Words				
torch	porch	sport	horse	storm
north	thorn	store	chore	score
shore	tore	oar	soar	board

or Words — fork	*ore* Words — more	*oar* Words — boar

Read, Spell, Read!

High Frequency/Tricky Words Read each word out loud. Touch under each letter in each word, spell the word out loud, and read the word again. Then read the sentence. Underline the word in each sentence. Write the answer to the question using the underlined word.

little — Grams wants just a little bit of cream in her tea. Nick went to get it for her.
What did Grams want in her tea?

sugar — Anne was out of sugar, but the storm kept her in the house. She hopes the rain will stop soon.
Why did Anne need to go to the store?

heard — Beth ran to get her mom when she heard the phone ring. It could be a call from her Mom's pal, Jean.
When did Beth go to get her mom?

Copyright © 2004 by High Noon Books. Permission granted to reproduce for classroom use.

Reading, Writing & Spelling

Name _____

Spelling Words

torch	porch	sport	horse	storm	north
thorn	store	chore	score	shore	tore
oar	soar	board	heard	little	sugar

Proofreading — Use proofreading marks to mark the errors in the sentences. Then rewrite the misspelled words with corrections on the lines provided.

Proofreading Marks
∧ Insert   ⋌ Delete   ◯ Check Spelling   ≡ Uppercase Needed

I heard the hail frum the starm pound down on the porch. Up the hill my hors trots for the barne. A loose bord from my gait just flew into the wind. I hop the storm will move up the shore by the time night comes, or I will not be able too drive up northe very soon.

List the correct spelling of the misspelled words below.

_____
_____

ending scor from the game was proof are team had realy lost. We did not soarr to the top as some had thought we would. Football was over for the year, and even though we were a little sad, the coach said each of us should be a good spart. after the toarch on the field was put out, we all went to Sugar Shack store for a quick snack.

List the correct spelling of the misspelled words below.

_____
_____

Name _____

Spelling Words

torch	sport	storm	north	thorn
store	chore	score	shore	tore
soar	board	little	heard	sugar

Crack the Code

Break the code to find your spelling words below.

st	c	ore	h	ear	ch	oar	sh	t	p
m	d	or	n	th	l	s	b	i	e

#		Break the code	Make the word
1.		p ch or	porch
2.			
3.			
4.			
5.			
6.			
7.			
8.			
9.			
10.			
11.			
12.			
13.			
14.			
15.			

Copyright © 2004 by High Noon Books. Permission granted to reproduce for classroom use.

Name

Fold the first column under. Take the Pretest and write your answers in the second column. Unfold and self-check your answers. Study the words and write corrections in the third column.

Spelling Words	Take the Pretest	Write Corrections
1. merge	1.	1.
2. perch	2.	2.
3. firm	3.	3.
4. skirt	4.	4.
5. blur	5.	5.
6. hurt	6.	6.
7. first	7.	7.
8. fern	8.	8.
9. swirl	9.	9.
10. burn	10.	10.
11. curl	11.	11.
12. girl	12.	12.
13. turn	13.	13.
14. clerk	14.	14.
15. herd	15.	15.
16. after	16.	16.
17. wear	17.	17.
18. guard	18.	18.

Challenge Words

19.	19.	19.
20.	20.	20.

➤ /ur/ is usually spelled *ir*, *ur*, or *er* as in *curb*, *bird*, or *swerve*.

Word Sort

Name _____

Pattern Words Use the key words below to help you sort each pattern word by the indicated pattern.

Pattern Words
merge   perch   fern   clerk   herd
firm   skirt   first   swirl   girl
blur   hurt   burn   curl   turn

er Words — her	*ir* Words — flirt	*ur* Words — burst

Read, Spell, Read!

High Frequency/Tricky Words Read each word out loud. Touch under each letter in each word, spell the word out loud, and read the word again. Then read the sentence. Underline the word in each sentence. Write the answer to the question using the underlined word.

after — Mike can't wait for after school. He wants to shop for a new bike!
When will Mike shop for a new bike?

guard — The man at the door is the same guard Pat saw there last night. He must work for the bank.
Who did Pat see at the door?

wear — Becky wants to wear the same pair of jeans to school each day. Her mom said yes, as long as they are clean.
Why did Becky ask her mom to wash her jeans?

25

Reading, Writing & Spelling

Name _____

Spelling Words

merge	perch	fern	clerk	herd
firm	skirt	first	swirl	girl
blur	hurt	burn	curl	turn

Fill in the Blank
For each line write the word from your spelling list that should fill in the blank.

1. I saw a small bird try to _____ on the limb of the tree.
2. The house will _____ down if the fire is not put out.
3. She wants to _____ her hair before she goes out.
4. The green _____ hung from the hook on the porch.
5. _____ the paint colors in one can to get the right shade.
6. _____ left at the next street to get to the mall.
7. Meg went to the store to buy a new _____.
8. I need to _____ into the next lane or I will miss the turn.
9. Bill did not get _____ when he fell out of the tree.
10. Rain on the glass made the road look like a _____.
11. The fruit still felt _____ when I gave it a squeeze.
12. We have a new _____ in our class.
13. It was time to feed the _____ of sheep.
14. The _____ at the desk was glad to have a job.

Word Building
Choose a spelling word you did not use above.

15. Which spelling word did you not use above? _____
16. Create new words from the letters of this word and list below:

_____

Name _____

Spelling Words

merge	perch	fern	clerk	herd	firm
skirt	first	swirl	girl	blur	hurt
burn	curl	turn	after	wear	guard

Exploring Words — Complete the chart. Choose letters or letter pairs to build a word from the spelling list. Or, fill in the missing parts of completed words. Circle the correct vowel spelling pattern.

SAMPLE							
Build the word.	f	er	ir	ur	m	=	firm
Find the missing parts.	cl	er	ir	ur	k	=	clerk

1.	p	er	ir	ur	ch	=	
2.		er	ir	ur		=	girl
3.	bl	er	ir	ur		=	
4.		er	ir	ur		=	fern
5.	m	er	ir	ur	ge	=	
6.	t	er	ir	ur	n	=	
7.		er	ir	ur		=	swirl
8.	sk	er	ir	ur	t	=	
9.		er	ir	ur		=	burn
10.		er	ir	ur		=	herd
11.	h	er	ir	ur	t	=	
12.		er	ir	ur		=	first
13.	c	er	ir	ur	l	=	

Complete the following **analogies** using spelling words from your list.

1. **Cake** is to **eat** as **skirt** is to _____.
2. **Up** is to **down** as **before** is to _____.
3. **Turn** is to **twirl** as **watch** is to _____.

Copyright © 2004 by High Noon Books. Permission granted to reproduce for classroom use.

Pretest

Name _____

Fold the first column under. Take the Pretest and write your answers in the second column. Unfold and self-check your answers. Study the words and write corrections in the third column.

Spelling Words	Take the Pretest	Write Corrections
1. haul	1.	1.
2. spoon	2.	2.
3. lawn	3.	3.
4. smooth	4.	4.
5. launch	5.	5.
6. stood	6.	6.
7. pool	7.	7.
8. cook	8.	8.
9. hawk	9.	9.
10. swoop	10.	10.
11. crook	11.	11.
12. room	12.	12.
13. vault	13.	13.
14. book	14.	14.
15. drawn	15.	15.
16. friend	16.	16.
17. hour	17.	17.
18. gauge	18.	18.
Challenge Words		
19.	19.	19.
20.	20.	20.

- /ŏŏ/ is usually spelled *oo* as in *look*.
- /ōō/ is usually spelled *oo* as in *moon*.
- /aw/ is sometimes spelled *au* or *aw* as in *fault* or *paw*.

28

Word Sort

Name _____

Pattern Words Use the key words below to help you sort each pattern word by the indicated pattern.

Pattern Words				
haul	launch	vault	lawn	hawk
drawn	spoon	smooth	pool	swoop
room	stood	cook	crook	book

au Words **fault**	*aw* Words **paw**	*oo* Words **moon**	*oo* Words **look**

Read, Spell, Read!

High Frequency/Tricky Words Read each word out loud. Touch under each letter in each word, spell the word out loud, and read the word again. Then read the sentence. Underline the word in each sentence. Write the answer to the question using the underlined word.

hour — The hour hand on the clock was on six when they left. For sure they will be late!
  Which clock hand was on six when they left?

_____

gauge — Matt's tire got flat as he rode down the hill. His mom had a tire gauge to help him know how much air the tire would take.
  What did Matt use to help put air in his tire?

_____

friend — Brad said he will go to camp if he can bring his friend James. He wants to have at least one pal on the trip.
  Who does Brad want to bring on the trip?

_____

Copyright © 2004 by High Noon Books. Permission granted to reproduce for classroom use.

Reading, Writing & Spelling

Name _____

Spelling Words

haul	launch	vault	lawn	hawk	drawn
spoon	smooth	pool	swoop	room	stood
cook	crook	book	friend	hour	gauge

Clues

Read the clues. Choose the spelling word that best fits the clue.

1. It rhymes with *book* and you do it to food. _____
2. This is the past tense of *stand*. _____
3. This is someone you know and like. _____
4. You do this when a boat leaves shore. _____
5. This means not rough. _____
6. You can read it. _____
7. This rhymes with *pawn* and starts like *dry*. _____
8. This helps you tell time. _____
9. Birds do this when they dive for food. _____
10. It rhymes with *page* and starts like *game*. _____
11. This is part of a building. _____
12. This is a place you lock up things in. _____
13. This is someone who steals things. _____
14. You do this when you take things away. _____

Each group of words below represents a category.
Find a spelling word that could be grouped with each category and write it on the line provided.

1. pond, lake, sea, creek _____
2. fork, plate, knife, glass _____
3. tree, bush, plant, flower _____
4. pig, fish, snake, bug _____

Word Play

Name _____

Spelling Words

haul	launch	vault	lawn	hawk	drawn
spoon	smooth	pool	swoop	room	stood
cook	crook	book	friend	hour	gauge

Word Find

Find the spelling words in the word find puzzle below. Circle each word.

Q	I	U	D	F	A	S	M	O	O	T	H	U	G	O	K	W	K	G	L
W	D	Y	A	R	H	U	X	V	B	M	O	D	E	A	S	C	I	A	X
C	E	L	C	V	A	S	P	M	Q	M	N	D	V	F	U	P	J	R	O
U	Y	A	R	Y	L	W	F	L	X	E	L	F	S	A	D	G	O	H	P
K	P	W	I	G	P	G	N	O	I	B	P	C	T	T	Y	L	E	A	O
P	K	N	H	J	E	J	K	R	T	V	R	O	O	M	P	N	S	W	M
C	A	O	P	P	H	L	F	F	Y	C	Q	S	O	W	E	X	D	K	I
D	R	Y	L	O	G	P	U	J	J	X	W	W	D	X	S	P	F	I	T
F	P	O	U	D	O	E	T	H	A	U	L	A	B	S	C	E	G	S	F
S	E	A	O	A	S	L	R	L	L	F	F	H	M	P	E	T	U	V	E
E	T	S	L	K	H	I	E	E	O	D	O	G	U	O	L	L	I	A	C
R	F	U	G	O	F	E	F	D	I	U	A	B	O	O	K	W	O	U	D
G	T	F	E	T	D	V	A	K	R	E	S	P	P	N	X	O	L	L	S
T	I	T	W	A	F	M	S	B	E	D	X	O	B	A	C	S	P	T	A
U	S	L	A	U	N	C	H	I	E	O	D	C	T	G	W	E	O	T	Q
K	W	U	G	J	G	L	R	A	R	P	Q	L	O	P	V	B	K	Y	W
O	E	L	E	U	I	F	P	Y	B	I	W	N	F	O	I	S	F	P	E
G	T	O	K	R	K	R	L	W	T	H	E	I	W	L	K	E	D	O	T
C	R	S	W	O	O	P	K	A	O	G	T	K	I	M	Q	F	A	K	F
V	V	W	E	T	H	W	G	T	H	R	O	U	G	H	A	C	W	C	V

Pretest

Name _____

Fold the first column under. Take the Pretest and write your answers in the second column. Unfold and self-check your answers. Study the words and write corrections in the third column.

Spelling Words	Take the Pretest	Write Corrections
1. braces	1.	1.
2. itches	2.	2.
3. roses	3.	3.
4. horses	4.	4.
5. classes	5.	5.
6. cases	6.	6.
7. pushes	7.	7.
8. teaches	8.	8.
9. dishes	9.	9.
10. places	10.	10.
11. dresses	11.	11.
12. causes	12.	12.
13. lunches	13.	13.
14. bridges	14.	14.
15. pieces	15.	15.
16. oh	16.	16.
17. aisles	17.	17.
18. heroes	18.	18.

Challenge Words

19.	19.	19.
20.	20.	20.

➤ To form the plural for most singular nouns, add –s.
➤ To form the plural of a noun that ends in s, ss, ch, sh, x, or z, add –es.

Word Sort

Name _____

Pattern Words Use the key words below to help you sort each pattern word by the indicated pattern.

Pattern Words				
braces	roses	horses	cases	places
causes	bridges	pieces	itches	classes
pushes	teaches	dishes	dresses	lunches

-s Words   cats

-es Words   bunches

Read, Spell, Read!

High Frequency/Tricky Words Read each word out loud. Touch under each letter in each word, spell the word out loud, and read the word again. Then read the sentence. Underline the word in each sentence. Write the answer to the question using the underlined word.

aisles The game was about to start, and the stands were full. People had to stand in the aisles.
   Where did people have to stand?

heroes Mr. Hill taught us about the war heroes at school. Next we will have to write about them in class.
   Who did the kids learn about at school?

oh I heard Jack jump and yell, "Oh no!" as the frame fell on the floor. At least the glass did not break!
   What did Jack yell when he dropped the frame?

Reading, Writing & Spelling

Name _____

Spelling Words

braces	roses	horses	cases	places
causes	bridges	pieces	itches	classes
pushes	teaches	dishes	dresses	lunches

Fill in the Blank
For each line write the word from your spelling list that should fill in the blank.

1. It is Steven's turn to wash the _____.
2. Sam needs to get _____ on his teeth soon.
3. How many _____ of gum do you have?
4. They need to take their _____ today for the trip.
5. If he _____ you down again, you need to tell me.
6. I have three _____ of food for the food bank.
7. I have to scratch because the bite _____.
8. The _____ are in bloom!
9. Bess loves to ride _____.
10. Becky has six _____ at her high school.
11. We all bought blue _____ for the dance.
12. There are five _____ we must see in Rome!
13. I have to cross two _____ on the way home.
14. The drum set always _____ lots of noise.

Word Building
Choose a spelling word you did not use above.

15. Which spelling word did you not use above? _____
16. Create new words from the letters of this word and list below:

_____

Word Play

Name _____

Spelling Words

braces	roses	horses	cases	places	causes
bridges	pieces	itches	classes	pushes	teaches
dishes	dresses	lunches	oh	aisles	heroes

Word Paths

Use a ruler to connect one letter from each row to the next to find all the letters in one of your spelling words. Then write the word on the line provided. Each letter should be used once.

B	U	A	C	E	E	S
T	R	C	C	H	S	
L	E	N	H	H	E	S
I	T	A	C	E	S	

1. _____
2. _____
3. _____
4. _____

C	R	I	S	G	E	
A	L	E	D	E	E	S
D	R	A	L	S	E	S
B	I	S	S	S	S	S

5. _____
6. _____
7. _____
8. _____

H	E	R	C	E	S
P	O	A	S	E	S
H	A	U	S	E	S
C	L	R	O	E	S

9. _____
10. _____
11. _____
12. _____

R	U	E	E	E	S
P	O	S		E	
O	I		C		S
P	H	S	H	S	

13. _____
14. _____
15. _____
16. _____

Pretest

Name _____

Fold the first column under. Take the Pretest and write your answers in the second column. Unfold and self-check your answers. Study the words and write corrections in the third column.

Spelling Words	Take the Pretest	Write Corrections
1. cheated	1.	1.
2. hoped	2.	2.
3. fainted	3.	3.
4. planted	4.	4.
5. raced	5.	5.
6. used	6.	6.
7. toasted	7.	7.
8. baked	8.	8.
9. melted	9.	9.
10. sounded	10.	10.
11. sneezed	11.	11.
12. dusted	12.	12.
13. bounced	13.	13.
14. started	14.	14.
15. scored	15.	15.
16. people	16.	16.
17. meant	17.	17.
18. niece	18.	18.

Challenge Words

19.	19.	19.
20.	20.	20.

➤ When a word ends in a silent *e*, drop the *e* before adding a suffix that begins with a vowel.
➤ Adding the suffix *-ed* to a word makes it past tense as in *cleaned*.

Word Sort

Name _____

Pattern Words Use the key words below to help you sort each pattern word by the indicated pattern.

Pattern Words
cheated fainted planted toasted melted
sounded dusted started hoped raced
used baked sneezed bounced scored

Words with -ed *painted*

Words with drop e + ed *laced*

Read, Spell, Read!

High Frequency/Tricky Words Read each word out loud. Touch under each letter in each word, spell the word out loud, and read the word again. Then read the sentence. Underline the word in each sentence. Write the answer to the question using the underlined word.

people — Three people came to their show. It was a very small crowd.
How many came to see the show?

meant — Pat made a clay pot in class and meant to glaze it before he left. The next time he comes to class he will need to do this.
What was Pat's plan that he did not do?

niece — Randy's niece plans to come over next week. She wants to see his new dog.
Who wants to see Randy's new pet?

Reading, Writing & Spelling

Name _____

Spelling Words

cheated	fainted	planted	toasted	melted
sounded	dusted	started	hoped	raced
used	baked	sneezed	bounced	scored

Writing — Last week you did a lot. Your mom and dad gave you lots of chores to do. Using at least five of your spelling words describe what you did.

_____
_____
_____
_____
_____
_____
_____
_____
_____

Check the following after you have proofread your writing.

☐ Check here if you proofread for **misspelled** words.
☐ Check here if you proofread for **words** you may have **left out** of your writing.
☐ Check here if you proofread for **punctuation**.
☐ Check here if you reread your writing to make sure it **makes sense**.

List below the spelling words from your list that you used in your writing.

_____
_____

List other words that were hard to spell. Proofread and check spellings.

_____
_____

LESSON 8 — Word Play

Name _____

Spelling Words

cheated	fainted	planted	toasted	melted	sounded
dusted	started	hoped	raced	used	bounced
sneezed	baked	scored	people	meant	niece

Crossword

Use the clues provided to fill in the crossword puzzle with your spelling words. Only use each word once.

Across
3. went fast
5. to pass out
10. air from nose and mouth
11. to have made points
12. not new
13. your sister's girl
14. to have moved up and down
15. changed by heat
16. to take dirt by wiping

Down
1. to have cooked
2. to have just begun
4. to have not told the truth
6. heated and made brown
7. girls and boys
8. to have put in the ground with dirt
9. to have wanted
10. made a noise
15. rhymes with tent

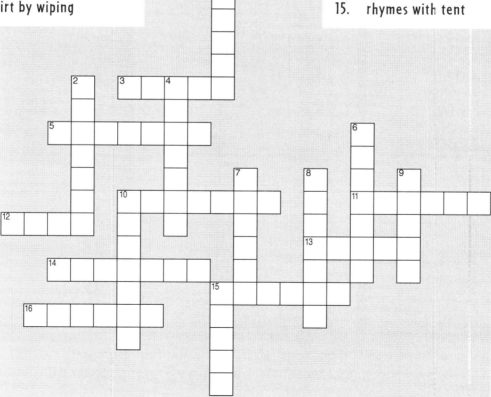

Copyright © 2004 by High Noon Books. Permission granted to reproduce for classroom use.

Name

Fold the first column under. Take the Pretest and write your answers in the second column. Unfold and self-check your answers. Study the words and write corrections in the third column.

Spelling Words	Take the Pretest	Write Corrections
1. braked	1.	1.
2. dipped	2.	2.
3. planned	3.	3.
4. trapped	4.	4.
5. saved	5.	5.
6. skipped	6.	6.
7. thinned	7.	7.
8. caged	8.	8.
9. slammed	9.	9.
10. nodded	10.	10.
11. faced	11.	11.
12. named	12.	12.
13. joked	13.	13.
14. judged	14.	14.
15. dripped	15.	15.
16. many	16.	16.
17. length	17.	17.
18. dealt	18.	18.

Challenge Words

19.	19.	19.
20.	20.	20.

➤ When you add a suffix to a CVC, short vowel word, double the final consonant.
➤ When a word ends in a silent *e*, drop the *e* before adding a suffix that begins with a vowel.
➤ Adding the suffix *-ed* to a word makes it past tense as in *baked*.

40

Copyright © 2004 by High Noon Books. Permission granted to reproduce for classroom use.

Word Sort

Name _____

Pattern Words Use the key words below to help you sort each pattern word by the indicated pattern.

Pattern Words
braked saved caged faced named
joked judged dipped planned trapped
skipped thinned slammed nodded dripped

Words with drop e + -ed *paved*

_____ _____
_____ _____
_____ _____
_____ _____

Words with doubling + -ed *pinned*

_____ _____
_____ _____
_____ _____
_____ _____

Read, Spell, Read!

High Frequency/Tricky Words Read each word out loud. Touch under each letter in each word, spell the word out loud, and read the word again. Then read the sentence. Underline the word in each sentence. Write the answer to the question using the underlined word.

many Becky plans to ask many people to come with her to the ball game. She paid for the seats at the park.
Who will go with Becky to the baseball game?

dealt The rules of the game say that five cards need to be dealt to each child. We will need to start over since we only have three cards each.
What are the rules of the game?

length The length of the sleeves on his new shirt is too long. He will need to take the shirt back to the store.
Why will he need to take the shirt back?

Reading, Writing & Spelling

Name _____

Spelling Words

braked	saved	caged	faced	named
joked	judged	dipped	planned	trapped
skipped	thinned	slammed	nodded	dripped

Proofreading — Use proofreading marks to mark the errors in the sentences. Then rewrite the misspelled words with corrections on the lines provided.

Proofreading Marks

∧ Insert   ⋏ Delete   ◯ Check Spelling   ≡ Uppercase Needed

   A slight noise coold be heard in the stret as Al brakeed to park the car by the house Rose skiped to the door to see if her Mom and dad were home. As she ran to see, the door slamed shut and locked her out! Now she was trapeed in the yard!

List the correct spelling of the misspelled words below.

_____

_____

   Her ice cream kone driped in the hot sun as Pam walked past the cagged birds at the zoo. She walked and jaked with her group. far away Pam could see Ann with her group. Just as Pam noded and waveed, ann turned and fased the bears. Pam would try to meat up with Ann at lunch to see if she was having fun

List the correct spelling of the misspelled words below.

_____

_____

42 Copyright © 2004 by High Noon Books. Permission granted to reproduce for classroom use.

LESSON 9 Word Play

Name _____

Spelling Words

braked	saved	caged	faced	named	joked
judged	dipped	planned	trapped	skipped	thinned
slammed	nodded	dripped	many	length	dealt

Exploring Words

Complete the chart. Choose base words or endings to build a word from the spelling list. You will need to *drop the e* or *double the consonant* at the end of the word.

SAMPLE

Drop the e by crossing it out.	hike		+	ed	=	hiked
Double the final consonant.	hop	p	+	ed	=	hopped

1.	brake		+	ed	=	
2.	dip		+	ed	=	
3.	slam		+	ed	=	
4.			+	ed	=	saved
5.	nod		+	ed	=	
6.	judge		+	ed	=	
7.	skip		+	ed	=	
8.			+	ed	=	planned
9.	name		+	ed	=	
10.			+	ed	=	dripped
11.			+	ed	=	trapped
12.	thin		+	ed	=	
13.	face		+	ed	=	

Complete the following **analogies** using spelling words from your list.

1. **New** is to **old** as **few** is to _____ .

2. **Trees** is to **planted** as **cards** is to _____ .

3. **Scale** is to **weight** as **ruler** is to _____ .

Copyright © 2004 by High Noon Books. Permission granted to reproduce for classroom use.

Pretest

Name _____

Fold the first column under. Take the Pretest and write your answers in the second column. Unfold and self-check your answers. Study the words and write corrections in the third column.

Spelling Words	Take the Pretest	Write Corrections
1. barking	1.	1.
2. rocking	2.	2.
3. hiding	3.	3.
4. hiking	4.	4.
5. knowing	5.	5.
6. playing	6.	6.
7. boring	7.	7.
8. snowing	8.	8.
9. baking	9.	9.
10. braking	10.	10.
11. brushing	11.	11.
12. cleaning	12.	12.
13. sleeping	13.	13.
14. feeling	14.	14.
15. climbing	15.	15.
16. every	16.	16.
17. yield	17.	17.
18. ceiling	18.	18.

Challenge Words

19.	19.	19.
20.	20.	20.

➤ When a word ends in a silent *e*, drop the *e* before adding a suffix that begins with a vowel.

➤ When the suffix *-ing* is added to a word, it sometimes makes the word a present participle verb or an adjective.

Word Sort

Name _____

Pattern Words Use the key words below to help you sort each pattern word by the indicated pattern.

Pattern Words

barking	rocking	knowing	playing	snowing
brushing	cleaning	sleeping	feeling	climbing
hiding	hiking	boring	baking	braking

Words with -ing   *talking*

_____
_____
_____
_____
_____
_____
_____
_____

Words with drop e + -ing   *racing*

_____
_____
_____
_____
_____
_____
_____
_____

Read, Spell, Read!

High Frequency/Tricky Words Read each word out loud. Touch under each letter in each word, spell the word out loud, and read the word again. Then read the sentence. Underline the word in each sentence. Write the answer to the question using the underlined word.

every — Every child will learn to read in class this year. There are lots of books in the room we will use.
   Who will learn to read this year?

yield — The sign by the curb told Dan to yield to other cars. That meant he had to wait for them to go first.
   What did the sign tell Dan to do?

ceiling — Ashley's ceiling is ten feet tall at her house. The set of shelves her dad built for her will all fit!
   What is ten feet tall at Ashley's house?

Copyright © 2004 by High Noon Books. Permission granted to reproduce for classroom use.

Reading, Writing & Spelling

Name _____

Spelling Words

barking	rocking	knowing	playing	snowing
brushing	cleaning	sleeping	feeling	climbing
hiding	hiking	boring	baking	braking

Dictionary & Vocabulary Connections

play (plā) v. played, playing, plays **1.** To have fun or sport with: *The children are playing.* **2.** To act in jest: *They are just playing around.* **3.** To act a role or part: *She will play a cat in the skit.*

1. Using the information above, what part or parts of speech is the word *playing*? _____

2. Using all definitions above, create a web of synonyms for *playing*. You can use words or phrases.

   (playing)

3. Which of the following could be the guide words for *play*? _____
   a. plate   playa   b. plasma   plat   c. plate   plastic

4. Use definition #2 above and write your own sentence using the word *playing*. _____

5. Use definition #3 above and write your own sentence using the word *playing*. _____

6. List up to three words from the spelling list that come before and after *playing* in the dictionary.

   Before   After

LESSON 10 — Word Play

Name _____

Spelling Words

barking	rocking	knowing	snowing	brushing
cleaning	sleeping	climbing	hiding	hiking
boring	baking	every	yield	ceiling

Crack the Code

Break the code to find your spelling words below.

Code key:
- e, mb, b, k, r, h, d, kn, ck, l, ay
- i_e, ore, ea, ie, er, v, y, o, s, ar, p
- ow, n, u, sh, c, a_e, ing, ee, i, ei, f

#	Break the code	Make the word
1.		
2.		
3.		
4.		
5.		
6.		
7.		
8.		
9.		
10.		
11.		
12.		
13.		
14.		
15.		

Copyright © 2004 by High Noon Books. Permission granted to reproduce for classroom use.

Pretest

Name _____

Fold the first column under. Take the Pretest and write your answers in the second column. Unfold and self-check your answers. Study the words and write corrections in the third column.

Spelling Words	Take the Pretest	Write Corrections
1. making	1.	1.
2. biking	2.	2.
3. shipping	3.	3.
4. sitting	4.	4.
5. spinning	5.	5.
6. racing	6.	6.
7. voting	7.	7.
8. shopping	8.	8.
9. saving	9.	9.
10. writing	10.	10.
11. diving	11.	11.
12. dripping	12.	12.
13. planning	13.	13.
14. batting	14.	14.
15. winning	15.	15.
16. before	16.	16.
17. skiing	17.	17.
18. lying	18.	18.

Challenge Words

19.	19.	19.
20.	20.	20.

➤ When you add a suffix to a CVC, short vowel word, double the final consonant before adding the suffix.
➤ When a word ends in a silent *e*, drop the *e* before adding a suffix that begins with a vowel.
➤ When the suffix *-ing* is added to a word, it sometimes makes the word a present participle verb or an adjective.

Word Sort

Pattern Words Use the key words below to help you sort each pattern word by the indicated pattern.

Pattern Words

shipping	sitting	spinning	shopping	dripping
planning	batting	winning	making	biking
racing	voting	saving	writing	diving

Words with doubling + -ing *tapping*

Words with drop e + -ing *driving*

_____

Read, Spell, Read!

High Frequency/Tricky Words Read each word out loud. Touch under each letter in each word, spell the word out loud, and read the word again. Then read the sentence. Underline the word in each sentence. Write the answer to the question using the underlined word.

skiing Ben told Mark the bus for the trip will leave school at noon. Mark needs to be on time, or he will not get to go skiing! What type of trip is Mark taking?

lying Juan found out that Sam had been lying to him about his friends. He now knew he could not trust Sam. What did Juan find out about Sam?

before Ron's dad told him he needed to brush his teeth before going to bed. He should not wait until morning. When did Ron's dad tell him to brush his teeth?

49

LESSON 11
Reading, Writing & Spelling

Name _____

Spelling Words

shipping	sitting	spinning	shopping	dripping
planning	batting	winning	making	biking
racing	voting	saving	writing	diving

Fill in the Blank For each line write the word from your spelling list that should fill in the blank.

1. I saw a man _____ off the cliff.

2. The _____ will soon take place at the poles.

3. James and Joe like to go _____ at the mall.

4. Mrs. Reese started _____ with a pen in class.

5. The _____ roll of the dice was ten.

6. Ben said you are _____ fifth in the game.

7. Sally is _____ her bike trip.

8. Have you been _____ your coins for a treat?

9. The store will be _____ the books to your home.

10. Chris likes to go _____ in the hills.

11. The cat was _____ on the fence.

12. Matt likes to play with the _____ top on the floor.

13. Kim was _____ down the street to catch the bus.

14. You could hear the water _____ in the sink.

Word Building Choose a spelling word you did not use above.

15. Which spelling word did you not use above? _____

16. Create new words from the letters of this word and list below:

_____

Word Play

Name _____

Spelling Words

shipping	sitting	spinning	shopping	dripping	planning
batting	winning	making	biking	racing	voting
saving	writing	diving	before	skiing	lying

Exploring Words — Complete the chart. Choose base words or endings to build a word from the spelling list. You will need to *drop the e* or *double the consonant* at the end of the word.

SAMPLE						
Drop the e by crossing it out.	mak~~e~~		+	ing	=	making
Double the final consonant.	ship	p	+	ing	=	shipping

1.			+	ing	=	saving
2.			+	ing	=	sitting
3.	plan		+	ing	=	
4.			+	ing	=	shopping
5.	vote		+	ing	=	
6.	bat		+	ing	=	
7.	spin		+	ing	=	
8.			+	ing	=	dripping
9.	bike		+	ing	=	
10.			+	ing	=	diving
11.			+	ing	=	racing
12.	write		+	ing	=	
13.	win		+	ing	=	

Complete the following **analogies** using spelling words from your list.

1. **Light** is to **dark** as **after** is to _____.
2. **Street** is to **driving** as **snow** is to _____.
3. **Chair** is to **sitting** as **couch** is to _____.

51

Pretest
LESSONS 6-11 REVIEW

Name _____

Fold the first column under. Take the Pretest and write your answers in the second column. Unfold and self-check your answers. Study the words and write corrections in the third column.

Spelling Words	Take the Pretest	Write Corrections
1. branches	1.	1.
2. heated	2.	2.
3. hugging	3.	3.
4. phoning	4.	4.
5. taping	5.	5.
6. sledded	6.	6.
7. burning	7.	7.
8. batted	8.	8.
9. glasses	9.	9.
10. squeezed	10.	10.
11. dreaming	11.	11.
12. laces	12.	12.
13. pointed	13.	13.
14. sipped	14.	14.
15. hitting	15.	15.
16. people	16.	16.
17. many	17.	17.
18. before	18.	18.

Challenge Words

| 19. | 19. | 19. |
| 20. | 20. | 20. |

➤ To form the plural for most singular nouns, add –s.
➤ To form the plural for a noun that ends in s, ss, ch, sh, x, or z, add –es.
➤ When you add a suffix to a CVC short vowel word, double the final consonant before adding the suffix.
➤ When a word ends in a silent e, drop the e before adding a suffix that begins with a vowel.
➤ Adding the suffix –ed to a word makes a past tense verb as in *floated*.

Name _____

Pattern Words Use the key words below to help you sort each pattern word by the indicated pattern.

Pattern Words

laces	burning	pages	branches	glasses
hoses	scratches	hugging	sledded	batted
sipped	hitting	phoning	taping	squeezed

-s Words	**roses**	-es Words	**classes**	Doubling + Suffix	**running**	Drop e + Suffix	**chasing**

Read, Spell, Read!

High Frequency/Tricky Words   Read each word out loud. Touch under each letter in each word, spell the word out loud, and read the word again. Then read the sentence. Underline the word in each sentence. Write the answer to the question using the underlined word.

people   People from towns far away came to watch the race. At the sound of the horn, they were off.
   Who came to watch the race?

_____

before   Pete has to do his chores before he can go to Tim's house. If he doesn't do them soon, it will be too late to go.
   When does Pete have to do his chores?

_____

many   Many boys tried out for the team, but only a few made the last cut. Rahul ran to check the list!
   Who tried out for the team?

_____

Copyright © 2004 by High Noon Books. Permission granted to reproduce for classroom use.

53

Name _____

Spelling Words

laces	hoses	pages	branches	glasses
laces	scratches	hugging	sledded	batted
sipped	hitting	phoning	taping	squeezed

Writing

Last night a huge storm came. There were no lights for most of the night. Using at least five of your spelling words, describe what your evening was like.

_____
_____
_____
_____
_____
_____
_____
_____
_____
_____

Check the following after you have proofread your writing.

☐ Check here if you proofread for **misspelled** words.
☐ Check here if you proofread for **words** you may have **left out** of your writing.
☐ Check here if you proofread for **punctuation**.
☐ Check here if you reread your writing to make sure it **makes sense**.

List below the spelling words from your list that you used in your writing.

_____
_____

List other words that were hard to spell. Proofread and check spellings.

_____
_____
_____

Word Play
LESSON 12 — LESSONS 6-11 REVIEW

Name _____

Spelling Words

branches	before	phoning	taping	sledded
burning	batted	glasses	dreaming	pointed
sipped	hitting	people	squeezed	many

Crack the Code

Break the code to find your spelling words below.

m	z	b	ph	p	a	ch	o_e	g	es
s	ur	squ	eo	d	l	r	h	ea	n	a_e
t	ed	ing	e	ss	ee	le	f	oi	y	ore

#	Break the code	Make the word
1. ★ ☺ □ 💻		
2. 💾 ☺ 💻 ✗ ☀ ∿		
3. ✈ ✋ ∿ ✗ 📖		
4. 💧 💾 ↗ □ 🕐		
5. 📁 ∿ ☺ 📁 👍		
6. ❄ ◆ □ 📁		
7. 🕐 ⌛ 🔔 🕐 ✈ 👍		
8. □ ☺ 💻 ☎		
9. ❄ ⌛ ❄ 👍 ♣		
10. ⌘ ✏ 🚩 👍		
11. 📪 ❄ ❄ ♥		
12. 💻 ✂ 📁 ❄ 👍		
13. ★ 🔔 ☺ ↗		
14. 📁 ♣ # 📁 □		
15. 💻 ✉ ↗ ∿		

Name _____

Fold the first column under. Take the Pretest and write your answers in the second column. Unfold and self-check your answers. Study the words and write corrections in the third column.

Spelling Words	Take the Pretest	Write Corrections
1. chilly	1.	1.
2. funny	2.	2.
3. muddy	3.	3.
4. rainy	4.	4.
5. chunky	5.	5.
6. sunny	6.	6.
7. foggy	7.	7.
8. sleepy	8.	8.
9. dirty	9.	9.
10. foamy	10.	10.
11. cloudy	11.	11.
12. sticky	12.	12.
13. lucky	13.	13.
14. blurry	14.	14.
15. witty	15.	15.
16. only	16.	16.
17. library	17.	17.
18. empty	18.	18.

Challenge Words

19.	19.	19.
20.	20.	20.

➤ When you add a suffix to a CVC short vowel word, double the final consonant before adding the suffix.
➤ Sometimes the suffix -y means *having the quality of* when added to a noun as in *foamy*.

Word Sort

Name _____

Pattern Words Use the key words below to help you sort each pattern word by the indicated pattern.

Pattern Words				
chilly	rainy	chunky	sleepy	dirty
foamy	cloudy	sticky	lucky	funny
muddy	sunny	foggy	blurry	witty

Words with -y *moody*

_____
_____
_____
_____
_____

Words with doubling + -y *saggy*

_____
_____
_____
_____
_____

Read, Spell, Read!

High Frequency/Tricky Words Read each word out loud. Touch under each letter in each word, spell the word out loud, and read the word again. Then read the sentence. Underline the word in each sentence. Write the answer to the question using the underlined word.

only The rules say you can only sing one song in the show and it must be short. That way more kids will have a chance to be on stage.
What are the rules for the show?

library Sandy found the new book Tad was asking about in the library on Fifth Street. The school library did not house it.
Where did Sandy find the new book?

empty The house looked empty as I watched my best friend drive away to his new home. I will really miss Samuel.
How did the house look?

Copyright © 2004 by High Noon Books. Permission granted to reproduce for classroom use.

LESSON 13

Reading, Writing & Spelling

Name _____

Spelling Words

chilly	rainy	chunky	sleepy	dirty
foamy	cloudy	sticky	lucky	funny
muddy	sunny	foggy	blurry	witty

Dictionary & Vocabulary Connections

sticky (stik•ē) *adj.* **1.** Having the property of sticking **2.** Covered with an adhesive agent: *a sticky lid* **3.** Warm: *a sticky day* **4.** Hard to do: *a sticky problem*

1. Using the information above, what part or parts of speech is the word *sticky?* _____

2. Using all definitions above, create a web of synonyms for *sticky*. You can use words or phrases.

   _____ ⟵ (sticky) ⟶ _____

   _____   _____

3. Which of the following could be the guide words for *sticky?* _____
   a. sting   stamp   b. stock   stoop   c. stick   still

4. Use definition #3 above and write your own sentence using the word *sticky*. _____

   _____

5. Use definition #4 above and write your own sentence using the word *sticky*. _____

   _____

   _____

6. List up to three words from the spelling list that come before and after *sticky* in the dictionary.

   Before   After

   _____   _____

   _____   _____

   _____   _____

58

Copyright © 2004 by High Noon Books. Permission granted to reproduce for classroom use.

Name _____

Spelling Words

chilly	rainy	chunky	sleepy	dirty	foamy
cloudy	sticky	lucky	funny	muddy	foggy
sunny	blurry	witty	empty	library	only

Word Paths — Connect one letter from each row to the next to find all the letters in one of your spelling words. Then write the word on the line provided. Each letter should be used once.

W	U	P	T	Y
L	I	T	K	Y
E	O	C	T	Y
F	M	A	M	Y

F	A	I	T	
O	U	L	N	Y
D	N	N	N	Y
R	I	R	Y	Y

B	H	E	E	R	Y
C	L	U	L	K	Y
S	T	I	R	P	Y
S	L	I	C	L	Y

C	U	O	G	K	Y
M	H	U	N	D	
F	L	G	D	Y	Y
C	O	D	U	Y	

1. _____
2. _____
3. _____
4. _____
5. _____
6. _____
7. _____
8. _____
9. _____
10. _____
11. _____
12. _____
13. _____
14. _____
15. _____
16. _____

Name _____

Fold the first column under. Take the Pretest and write your answers in the second column. Unfold and self-check your answers. Study the words and write corrections in the third column.

Spelling Words	Take the Pretest	Write Corrections
1. berries	1.	1.
2. married	2.	2.
3. bunnies	3.	3.
4. marries	4.	4.
5. carried	5.	5.
6. pennies	6.	6.
7. carries	7.	7.
8. worried	8.	8.
9. jellied	9.	9.
10. hurried	10.	10.
11. copies	11.	11.
12. hobbies	12.	12.
13. copied	13.	13.
14. kitties	14.	14.
15. worries	15.	15.
16. above	16.	16.
17. chief	17.	17.
18. ninth	18.	18.

Challenge Words

19.	19.	19.
20.	20.	20.

➤ When a word ends with a consonant and *y*, change the *y* to *i* before adding *-es* or *-ed*.
➤ Adding *-es* to a word makes it plural.
➤ Adding the suffix *-ed* to a word makes it past tense, as in *hurried*.

Word Sort

Name _____

Pattern Words Use the key words below to help you sort each pattern word by the indicated pattern.

Pattern Words				
berries	bunnies	marries	pennies	carries
copies	hobbies	kitties	worries	married
carried	worried	jellied	hurried	copied

Words with -ies   *bellies*

Words with -ied   *scurried*

Read, Spell, Read!

High Frequency/Tricky Words Read each word out loud. Touch under each letter in each word, spell the word out loud, and read the word again. Then read the sentence. Underline the word in each sentence. Write the answer to the question using the underlined word.

above It was getting dark in the woods, but above the tree tops Meg could still see a hawk soar. Soon the sky would be too black to see at all.
  Where did Meg see the hawk?

ninth Sam scored a run in the ninth inning of the game. The score was now 1 to 0.
  When did Sam score?

chief The chief needs to make sure all his men are ready to fight fires. They need to study and learn more each day.
  Who needs to make sure the men are ready?

Copyright © 2004 by High Noon Books. Permission granted to reproduce for classroom use.

61

Reading, Writing & Spelling

Name _____

Spelling Words

berries	bunnies	marries	pennies	carries
copies	hobbies	kitties	worries	married
carried	worried	jellied	hurried	copied

Clues
Read the clues. Choose the spelling word that best fits the clue.

1. These are baby cats. _____
2. This means to have rushed. _____
3. This starts like *corn* and ends like *hurried*. _____
4. When a man gets a wife he is this. _____
5. This means taking something to a place. _____
6. These are coins. _____
7. These are pets that hop. _____
8. This rhymes with *berries* and starts like *moth*. _____
9. Things you like to do when you have time. _____
10. This rhymes with *married* and starts like *coin*. _____
11. These can be thoughts you don't like. _____
12. These are more than one of something. _____
13. This means you did what someone else did. _____
14. These grow on a bush and are good to eat. _____

Each group of words below represents a category.
Find a spelling word that could be grouped with each category and write it on the line provided.

1. marry, marries _____
2. jelly, jellies _____
3. carry, carried _____
4. copy, copied _____

Name _____

Word Play

Spelling Words

berries	bunnies	marries	pennies	carries
copies	hobbies	kitties	worries	married
carried	worried	jellied	hurried	copied

Word Find

Find the spelling words in the word find puzzle below. Circle each word.

W	N	Y	P	G	W	C	N	M	A	R	R	I	E	S	R	C	H
F	C	H	I	E	F	H	A	D	I	T	C	A	V	H	H	O	O
I	H	A	P	E	N	N	I	E	S	R	H	I	K	E	I	P	P
H	O	B	B	I	E	S	T	N	W	O	R	R	I	E	S	I	H
E	C	O	A	V	M	H	C	O	H	T	J	K	L	D	H	E	E
N	H	V	R	O	U	O	H	A	A	H	I	M	E	O	C	D	B
A	V	E	K	Y	B	C	B	E	R	R	I	E	S	J	A	R	C
M	O	W	D	U	R	H	U	D	N	R	G	F	R	E	R	P	N
B	A	O	R	C	A	I	N	O	B	E	I	O	E	K	R	K	O
R	F	R	O	O	H	L	N	T	I	P	L	E	T	O	I	E	N
A	V	R	R	P	R	I	I	Y	K	O	K	D	S	B	E	V	X
R	T	I	A	I	O	B	E	W	L	Y	E	E	H	R	D	A	M
E	B	E	M	E	E	R	S	H	O	I	D	B	U	E	H	M	I
Y	O	D	E	S	B	D	T	I	R	B	R	O	D	T	A	I	B
E	H	A	B	E	R	W	H	R	A	E	L	N	N	H	I	N	R
K	I	T	T	I	E	S	U	A	N	K	O	I	A	E	N	M	O
E	B	O	H	H	W	H	A	R	G	E	N	B	S	U	L	E	J
R	A	H	I	S	P	J	Z	J	E	L	L	I	E	D	M	C	X

Name _____

Fold the first column under. Take the Pretest and write your answers in the second column. Unfold and self-check your answers. Study the words and write corrections in the third column.

Spelling Words	Take the Pretest	Write Corrections
1. brighter	1.	1.
2. greatest	2.	2.
3. hotter	3.	3.
4. maddest	4.	4.
5. brightest	5.	5.
6. biggest	6.	6.
7. weakest	7.	7.
8. smartest	8.	8.
9. deeper	9.	9.
10. wettest	10.	10.
11. thicker	11.	11.
12. meanest	12.	12.
13. dimmer	13.	13.
14. greenest	14.	14.
15. cleaner	15.	15.
16. better	16.	16.
17. seize	17.	17.
18. siege	18.	18.
Challenge Words		
19.	19.	19.
20.	20.	20.

➤ When you add a suffix to a CVC, short vowel word, double the final consonant before adding the suffix.
➤ The suffix *-er* and *-est* sometimes make a word comparative, as in *brighter*.

Word Sort

Name _____

Pattern Words Use the key words below to help you sort each pattern word by the indicated pattern.

Pattern Words				
brighter	hotter	deeper	thicker	dimmer
cleaner	greatest	maddest	brightest	biggest
weakest	smartest	wettest	meanest	greenest

Words with -er smarter

_____ _____
_____ _____
_____ _____
_____ _____

Words with -est cleanest

_____ _____
_____ _____
_____ _____
_____ _____

Read, Spell, Read!

High Frequency/Tricky Words Read each word out loud. Touch under each letter in each word, spell the word out loud, and read the word again. Then read the sentence. Underline the word in each sentence. Write the answer to the question using the underlined word.

better — Matt is better at playing golf than Rob, but Rob is better than Al. If there is room on the course they will all play at noon.
  Who is Rob better than?

seize — The knight tried to seize the sword during the fight. When it fell he ran to grab it.
  What did the knight try to do during the fight?

siege — The troops made a siege on the town. None of the town people could get away.
  What did the troops do to the town?

65

Reading, Writing & Spelling

Name _____

Spelling Words

brighter	hotter	deeper	thicker	dimmer
cleaner	greatest	maddest	brightest	biggest
weakest	smartest	wettest	meanest	greenest

Proofreading — Use proofreading marks to mark the errors in the sentences. Then rewrite the misspelled words with corrections on the lines provided.

Proofreading Marks
∧ Insert   ⋋ Delete   ◯ Check Spelling   ≡ Uppercase Needed

Sam wants to plant a peech tree next to the porch. he bot the greenes and bigest one he could find. The ferst whole he dug just wasn't deep enouf, so he plans to dig a deepir hole this afternoon.

List the correct spelling of the misspelled words below.

_____
_____

Yes it will be a beter night to spot the meny stars in the sky. Last night we were only able to sea the britest star in the east and it got dimer as the night went on.

List the correct spelling of the misspelled words below.

_____
_____

Lesson 15 · Word Play

Name _____

Spelling Words

brighter	hotter	deeper	thicker	dimmer	cleaner
greatest	maddest	brightest	biggest	weakest	smartest
wettest	meanest	greenest	better	seize	siege

Crossword

Use the clues provided to fill in the crossword puzzle with your spelling words. Only use each word once.

Across
4. has more light and shines more
7. not thinner
9. the most not dry
10. lacking the most strength
11. more far down
12. the most sharp mind
14. the most mad
16. to block a city

Down
1. the largest in size
2. the most green
3. rhymes with letter
5. very large in size
6. gives off more heat
8. more free of dirt
13. to grasp
14. the most cruel
15. not as bright

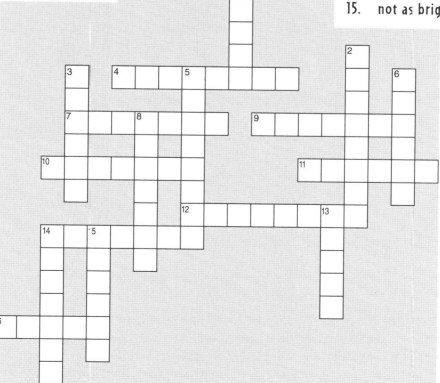

Name _____

Fold the first column under. Take the Pretest and write your answers in the second column. Unfold and self-check your answers. Study the words and write corrections in the third column.

Spelling Words	Take the Pretest	Write Corrections
1. dustier	1.	1.
2. safer	2.	2.
3. happiest	3.	3.
4. luckiest	4.	4.
5. safest	5.	5.
6. ruder	6.	6.
7. happier	7.	7.
8. palest	8.	8.
9. latest	9.	9.
10. funniest	10.	10.
11. nicer	11.	11.
12. funnier	12.	12.
13. cuter	13.	13.
14. nicest	14.	14.
15. cutest	15.	15.
16. mother	16.	16.
17. truly	17.	17.
18. family	18.	18.
Challenge Words 19.	19.	19.
20.	20.	20.

➤ When a word ends in a silent *e*, drop the *e* before adding a suffix that begins with a vowel.
➤ When a word ends in a consonant + *y*, you usually change the *y* to *i* before adding a suffix.
➤ The suffixes *–er* and *–est* sometimes make a word comparative, as in *later* or *latest*.

Word Sort

Name _____

Pattern Words Use the key words below to help you sort each pattern word by the indicated pattern.

Pattern Words

dustier	safer	happiest	luckiest	safest
ruder	happier	palest	latest	funniest
nicer	funnier	cuter	nicest	cutest

Words with drop e + -er *closer*	Words with -ier *luckier*	Words with drop e + -est *closest*	Words with -iest *dustiest*

Read, Spell, Read!

High Frequency/Tricky Words Read each word out loud. Touch under each letter in each word, spell the word out loud, and read the word again. Then read the sentence. Underline the word in each sentence. Write the answer to the question using the underlined word.

mother — Sara's mother brought home a new puppy. Joe's mother bought him a new bike.
 Who bought the new bike?

truly — Megan told a lie about her teacher. The next day she wrote a note saying she was truly sorry and took it to class for Mrs. Eck.
 What did Megan's note say?

family — George went to the park with his sister. Mark's whole family came with him to the picnic.
 Who went with Mark to the park?

Copyright © 2004 by High Noon Books. Permission granted to reproduce for classroom use.

Reading, Writing & Spelling

Name _____

Spelling Words

safer	ruder	nicer	cuter	dustier	happier
funnier	safest	palest	latest	nicest	cutest
happiest	luckiest	funniest	mother	truly	family

Clues
Read the clues. Choose the spelling word that best fits the clue.

1. This has the word *ice* in it and ends like *her*. _____
2. This means the best looking. _____
3. You might call your best friend this. _____
4. This means looks more cute than others. _____
5. This means the last one there. _____
6. This means the most free from risk. _____
7. This starts like *trust* and ends like *slowly*. _____
8. It is the most fun. _____
9. This is the most light in color. _____
10. Lacking grace more than others. _____
11. It means having more dirt on it. _____
12. If you are kept from harm more than others. _____
13. You are this if more good things happen to you. _____
14. This is having the most joy. _____

Each group of words below represents a category.
Find a spelling word that could be grouped with each category and write it on the line provided.

1. funny, funniest _____
2. happiest, happy _____
3. father, sister _____
4. group, unit _____

Word Play

Name _____

Spelling Words

safer	ruder	nicer	cuter	dustier	happier
funnier	safest	palest	latest	nicest	cutest
happiest	luckiest	funniest	mother	truly	family

Crack the Code

Break the code to find your spelling words below.

| d 📁 | u ✏️ | a 👍 | t 📫 | f ❄️ | h 👓 | p ☎️ | ck 📖 | c 🔔 | n ✋ |
| est ⏳ | er ★ | iest 🚩 | ier 🕐 | s ✈️ | a_e ✂️ | r ⌘ | u_e 💧 | l 💻 | i_e ✉️ |

	Break the code	Make the word
1. 📫✈️🕐📁✏️		
2. ☎️👓🚩👍☎️		
3. ✋❄️✋✏️🚩		
4. 📫💧★🔔		
5. ❄️⏳✂️✈️		
6. ✋⏳✉️🔔		
7. 📁⌘★💧		
8. ✋🔔✉️★		
9. ✏️🚩💻📖		
10. ✂️❄️★✈️		
11. ⏳💻📫✂️		
12. 🕐☎️👍☎️👓		
13. ✋❄️🕐✋✏️		
14. ✂️☎️⏳💻		
15. 💧📫⏳🔔		

Copyright © 2004 by High Noon Books. Permission granted to reproduce for classroom use.

71

Name

Fold the first column under. Take the Pretest and write your answers in the second column. Unfold and self-check your answers. Study the words and write corrections in the third column.

Spelling Words	Take the Pretest	Write Corrections
1. railroad	1.	1.
2. yourself	2.	2.
3. airport	3.	3.
4. bathroom	4.	4.
5. snowball	5.	5.
6. toothbrush	6.	6.
7. downstairs	7.	7.
8. highway	8.	8.
9. playground	9.	9.
10. somewhere	10.	10.
11. earthquake	11.	11.
12. flashlight	12.	12.
13. cardboard	13.	13.
14. necklace	14.	14.
15. snowflake	15.	15.
16. father	16.	16.
17. quiet	17.	17.
18. quite	18.	18.

Challenge Words

19.	19.	19.
20.	20.	20.

➤ A compound word is made up of two words joined together to make one word.

Name _____

Pattern Words Use the key words below to help you sort each pattern word by the indicated pattern.

Pattern Words

railroad	melted	reaches	downstairs	toothbrush
airport	snowball	speeding	somewhere	clapping
necklace	highway	splashes	flashlight	cardboard

Words with endings *reading*

_____ _____
_____ _____
_____ _____
_____ _____

Compound Words *baseball*

_____ _____
_____ _____
_____ _____
_____ _____

Read, Spell, Read!

High Frequency/Tricky Words Read each word out loud. Touch under each letter in each word, spell the word out loud, and read the word again. Then read the sentence. Underline the word in each sentence. Write the answer to the question using the underlined word.

father Everyone got to bring a guest to school for lunch. Marie brought her aunt. Sam brought his father.
    Who did Sam bring?
_____

quiet Ben said we all have to quiet down. We don't want to be sent out of the pet store.
    What did Ben say they had to do?
_____

quite When Dad came home he said, "I had quite a day at work!" He went on to say he had won a trip for two to Spain!
    What did Dad first say when he came in the house?
_____

Copyright © 2004 by High Noon Books. Permission granted to reproduce for classroom use.

73

LESSON 17 — Reading, Writing & Spelling

Name _____

Pattern Words

railroad	yourself	bathroom	downstairs	toothbrush
airport	snowball	snowflake	somewhere	playground
necklace	highway	flashlight	earthquake	cardboard

Writing

You can go on a trip anywhere. Where would you go, and what would you do?
Use at leat five of your spelling words in your writing below.

_____

_____

_____

_____

_____

_____

_____

_____

_____

_____

_____

Check the following after you have proofread your writing.

☐ Check here if you proofread for **misspelled** words.
☐ Check here if you proofread for **words** you may have **left out** of your writing.
☐ Check here if you proofread for **punctuation.**
☐ Check here if you reread your writing to make sure it **makes sense.**

List below the spelling words from your list that you used in your writing.

_____

_____

List other words that were hard to spell.

_____

_____

Word Play

Name _____

Pattern Words

railroad	flashlight	downstairs	earthquake	yourself	airport
snowball	snowflake	somewhere	playground	necklace	highway
father	bathroom	cardboard	toothbrush	quiet	quite

Crossword

Use the clues provided to fill in the crossword puzzle with your spelling words. Only use each word once.

Across
2. a ball made of something wet
4. it's stiff and made of pulp
6. rhymes with might
7. worn around your neck
10. a place where planes are
11. it shines a bright light
12. same as dad
13. not loud
16. cars drive on this
17. a place not known
18. kids play there

Down
1. meaning you
3. a place you take a bath
5. not upstairs
8. when the ground shakes
9. a flake of wet ice
14. cleans your teeth
15. a train uses this

Pretest
LESSONS 13-17
REVIEW

Name _____

Fold the first column under. Take the Pretest and write your answers in the second column. Unfold and self-check your answers. Study the words and write corrections in the third column.

Spelling Words	Take the Pretest	Write Corrections
1. blacker	1.	1.
2. fastest	2.	2.
3. luckier	3.	3.
4. bigger	4.	4.
5. rudest	5.	5.
6. closer	6.	6.
7. tamest	7.	7.
8. madder	8.	8.
9. dimmest	9.	9.
10. dustiest	10.	10.
11. wetter	11.	11.
12. later	12.	12.
13. luckiest	13.	13.
14. greater	14.	14.
15. cleanest	15.	15.
16. better	16.	16.
17. mother	17.	17.
18. father	18.	18.

Challenge Words

19.	19.	19.
20.	20.	20.

➤ When you add a suffix to a CVC short vowel word, double the final consonant before adding the suffix.
➤ When a word ends in a silent *e*, drop the *e* before adding a suffix that begins with a vowel.
➤ When a word ends in a consonant + *y*, you usually change the *y* to *i* before adding a suffix.
➤ The suffixes *-er* and *-est* sometimes make a word comparative, as in *bigger* or *biggest*.

Copyright © 2004 by High Noon Books. Permission granted to reproduce for classroom use.

Word Sort — Lessons 13-17 Review

Name _____

Pattern Words Use the key words below to help you sort each pattern word by the indicated pattern.

Pattern Words

fastest	greater	closer	cleanest	bigger
madder	dimmest	luckier	wetter	rudest
tamest	later	luckiest	dustiest	blacker

Words + Suffix — smartest	Words with doubling + Suffix — hotter	Words with drop e + Suffix — nicer	Words with y changed to i + Suffix — funnier

Read, Spell, Read!

High Frequency/Tricky Words Read each word out loud. Touch under each letter in each word, spell the word out loud, and read the word again. Then read the sentence. Underline the word in each sentence. Write the answer to the question using the underlined word.

better Ron did better than Jake on the math test. He spent more time on part one and less on part two.
    Who had the better score on the test?

mother Dan's mother made lunch for Joe and him at noon. Matt came later at three and had cake.
    Who made lunch?

father A pipe broke under the sink. Pam's father is good with tools. He can fix it!
    Who can fix the sink?

Name _____

Spelling Words

fastest	greater	closer	cleanest	bigger
madder	dimmest	luckier	wetter	rudest
tamest	later	luckiest	dustiest	blacker

Fill in the Blank
For each line write the word from your spelling list that should fill in the blank.

1. I cleaned the _____ shelf in the room.
2. Jim is _____ than I am at finding lost change.
3. Mike got _____ than Tom in the storm.
4. Yi has the _____ desk in class.
5. Four is _____ than three.
6. Pam is the _____ on the team, and she won the race.
7. I will stop by your house _____ on my way home.
8. Your dog is _____ than my puppy.
9. Juan's flashlight was the _____ when they turned it on.
10. Rex was the _____ bear I saw at the zoo.
11. Rosa's hair is _____ than Ann's hair.
12. The _____ day of Todd's life was when he won a prize!
13. Mom was _____ than I ever thought she would be!
14. Joe said the _____ thing and made everyone mad.

Word Building
Choose a spelling word you did not use above.

15. Which spelling word did you not use above? _____
16. Create new words from the letters of this word and list below:
    _____

78
Copyright © 2004 by High Noon Books. Permission granted to reproduce for classroom use.

Word Play
LESSONS 13-17
REVIEW

Name _____

Spelling Words

fastest	greater	closer	cleanest	bigger	madder
dimmest	luckier	wetter	rudest	tamest	later
luckiest	dustiest	blacker	better	mother	father

Exploring Words — Complete the chart. Before adding *er* or *est* to the base word to build a word from the spelling list determine if you need to *drop the e*, *change the y to i*, or *double the consonant* at the end of the word.

SAMPLE						
Drop the e by crossing it out.	rud~~e~~		+	est	=	rudest
Double the final consonant.	hot	t	+	est	=	hottest
Change the y to i and add er.	funn~~y~~	i	+	er	=	funnier

1.	tame		+	est	=	
2.	mad			er	=	
3.			+	er	=	luckier
4.			+	er	=	wetter
5.			+	est	=	fastest
6.	black		+	er	=	
7.			+	er	=	greater
8.	late		+	er	=	
9.			+	er	=	bigger
10.	dusty		+	est	=	
11.	clean		+	est	=	
12.	dim		+	est	=	

Complete the following **analogies** using spelling words from your list.

1. **More** is to **fewer** as **worse** is to _____ .
2. **Calf** is to **cow** as **child** is to _____ .
3. **Aunt** is to **mother** as **uncle** is to _____ .

Pretest

Name _____

Fold the first column under. Take the Pretest and write your answers in the second column. Unfold and self-check your answers. Study the words and write corrections in the third column.

Spelling Words	Take the Pretest	Write Corrections
1. untie	1.	1.
2. dislike	2.	2.
3. disturb	3.	3.
4. unclean	4.	4.
5. unlike	5.	5.
6. discount	6.	6.
7. unpack	7.	7.
8. distrust	8.	8.
9. unwrap	9.	9.
10. disrupt	10.	10.
11. display	11.	11.
12. unknown	12.	12.
13. dissect	13.	13.
14. unlock	14.	14.
15. dissolve	15.	15.
16. very	16.	16.
17. usage	17.	17.
18. usually	18.	18.

Challenge Words

19.	19.	19.
20.	20.	20.

➤ The prefix *un–* added to a root or base word usually means *not*.
➤ The prefix *dis–* added to a root or base word usually means *not* or *opposite of*.

Word Sort

Name _____

Pattern Words Use the key words below to help you sort each pattern word by the indicated pattern.

Pattern Words				
untie	dislike	disturb	unclean	unlike
discount	unpack	distrust	unwrap	disrupt
display	unknown	dissect	unlock	dissolve

Words with un- — unsure

_____ _____
_____ _____
_____ _____
_____ _____

Words with dis- — disagree

_____ _____
_____ _____
_____ _____
_____ _____

Read, Spell, Read!

High Frequency/Tricky Words Read each word out loud. Touch under each letter in each word, spell the word out loud, and read the word again. Then read the sentence. Underline the word in each sentence. Write the answer to the question using the underlined word.

very — Meg felt very sad when her dog, Sam, got sick. Sam had to stay at the vet for a whole week!
How did Meg feel when Sam was at the vet?

usage — Dad said we will get more usage from the new heated pool. The old one was too cold.
What did Dad say about the new pool?

usually — Last night they all got home at ten. Rob usually goes to sleep at nine, so this was late for him to be up.
When does Rob go to sleep?

Copyright © 2004 by High Noon Books. Permission granted to reproduce for classroom use.

Reading, Writing & Spelling

Name _____

Spelling Words

untie	dislike	disturb	unclean	unlike
discount	unpack	distrust	unwrap	disrupt
display	unknown	very	unlock	dissolve

Proofreading — Use proofreading marks to mark the errors in the sentences. Then rewrite the misspelled words with corrections on the lines provided.

Proofreading Marks
∧ Insert   ⁁ Delete   ◯ Check Spelling   ≡ Uppercase Needed

todd usually gets a descount at the stor where his Dad works. He was vary happy when he saw a shirt on displae that he liked. He had to wait for the clerk since he did not want to disterb her while she was waiting on someone else

List the correct spelling of the misspelled words below.

Rose had to unlok the front door befor she could bring in her suitcase from the trunk of the car. she put her bag on the bed as she started to unpac Rose tried not to disberb her pet rat who was sleeping by her bed.

List the correct spelling of the misspelled words below.

Word Play

Spelling Words

untie	dislike	disturb	unclean	unlike	discount
unpack	distrust	unwrap	disrupt	display	unknown
dissect	unlock	dissolve	very	usage	usually

Word Paths — Use a ruler to connect one letter from each row to the next to find all the letters in one of your spelling words. Then write the word on the line provided. Each letter should be used once.

U	N	T	O	A	P
U	N	A	G	E	
U	S	W	I	E	
U	N	L	R	C	K

1. _____
2. _____
3. _____
4. _____

D	N	U	P	U	A	N
U	I	C	A	L	R	Y
D	S	S	T	E	L	B
U	I	S	L	L	A	Y

5. _____
6. _____
7. _____
8. _____

U	I	P	R	K	P	
U	N	S	I	U	K	T
D	I	L	A	C	C	
D	N	S	S	E	E	T

9. _____
10. _____
11. _____
12. _____

U	I	K	C	R	K	N	T
D	N	S	L	I	W	S	
D	I	S	N	O	U	E	T
D	I	S	T	O	U	N	

13. _____
14. _____
15. _____
16. _____

Pretest

Name _____

Fold the first column under. Take the Pretest and write your answers in the second column. Unfold and self-check your answers. Study the words and write corrections in the third column.

Spelling Words	Take the Pretest	Write Corrections
1. unkind	1.	1.
2. reheat	2.	2.
3. remind	3.	3.
4. repeat	4.	4.
5. respond	5.	5.
6. reprint	6.	6.
7. return	7.	7.
8. react	8.	8.
9. unreal	9.	9.
10. unseen	10.	10.
11. unpaid	11.	11.
12. repair	12.	12.
13. reread	13.	13.
14. undress	14.	14.
15. retreat	15.	15.
16. sure	16.	16.
17. guess	17.	17.
18. hoarse	18.	18.
Challenge Words		
19.	19.	19.
20.	20.	20.

➤ The prefix *un–* added to a root or base word usually means *not*.
➤ The prefix *re–* added to a root or base word means *back* or *again*.

84

Copyright © 2004 by High Noon Books. Permission granted to reproduce for classroom use.

Word Sort

Name _____

Pattern Words Use the key words below to help you sort each pattern word by the indicated pattern.

Pattern Words

unkind	reheat	remind	repeat	respond
reprint	return	react	unreal	unseen
unpaid	repair	reread	undress	retreat

Words with un-   *undo*

_____ _____
_____ _____
_____ _____
_____ _____
_____ _____

Words with re-   *resend*

_____ _____
_____ _____
_____ _____
_____ _____
_____ _____

Read, Spell, Read!

High Frequency/Tricky Words Read each word out loud. Touch under each letter in each word, spell the word out loud, and read the word again. Then read the sentence. Underline the word in each sentence. Write the answer to the question using the underlined word.

sure Sal's mom said Lam was not sure he could give her a ride home this week. She will ask Tad if he can drive her.
Why did Sal's mom ask Tad for a ride?

guess Kim was told not to guess on her math test. She had to show her work or the teacher would return the test to her to redo.
What was Kim told not to do?

horse The pig found a place in the barn to sleep. The horse had a stall by the door, but the barn cats stayed out all night.
Who slept in the barn?

Copyright © 2004 by High Noon Books. Permission granted to reproduce for classroom use.

Reading, Writing & Spelling

LESSON 20

Name _____

Spelling Words

unkind	reheat	remind	repeat	respond
reprint	return	react	unreal	unseen
unpaid	repair	reread	undress	retreat

Dictionary & Vocabulary Connections

return (ri•tûrn) v. **1.** To send, put, or carry back: *Please return my shirt to me.* n. **2.** A thing brought or sent back: *The return was put back on the shelf.* **3.** A report on a vote: *The return from the election was not in yet.*

1. Using the information above, what part or parts of speech is the word *return?* _____

2. Using all definitions above, create a web of synonyms for *return.* You can use words or phrases.

   _____ →   ← _____

   (return)

   _____ →   ← _____

3. Which of the following could be the guide words for *return?* _____
   a. rose   rest   b. revive   revolt   c. retro   revamp

4. Use definition #1 above and write your own sentence using the word *return.* _____

   _____

5. Use definition #2 above and write your own sentence using the word *return.* _____

   _____

6. List up to three words from the spelling list that come before and after *return* in the dictionary.

   Before   After

   _____   _____

   _____   _____

   _____   _____

86   Copyright © 2004 by High Noon Books. Permission granted to reproduce for classroom use.

Word Play

Name _____

Spelling Words

unkind	reheat	remind	repeat	respond	reprint
return	react	unreal	unseen	unpaid	repair
reread	undress	retreat	guess	hoarse	sure

Word Find

Find the spelling words in the word find puzzle below. Circle each word.

L	R	P	S	E	R	I	R	E	P	R	I	N	T	T	R	U	U	I
T	R	E	E	D	E	N	S	I	I	L	R	A	D	E	O	L	T	S
S	U	R	A	M	E	R	K	P	U	N	R	E	A	L	R	S	M	E
P	R	U	U	C	R	U	N	P	A	I	D	G	R	R	T	R	K	A
C	C	T	N	N	T	E	E	S	L	E	N	A	S	U	R	E	S	E
I	P	R	R	S	K	T	P	S	L	R	P	I	A	P	R	U	S	O
N	D	A	E	A	E	N	E	E	S	R	E	S	P	O	N	D	E	N
D	R	T	P	R	R	E	A	R	U	R	E	E	T	U	I	N	U	N
R	E	N	E	E	E	G	N	D	A	E	E	S	A	A	R	I	G	E
R	I	S	A	E	S	A	S	N	K	E	I	T	E	S	U	K	N	P
T	A	A	T	C	E	I	D	U	S	R	A	E	R	R	C	N	J	F
R	S	S	P	E	E	S	S	R	R	E	C	R	T	N	P	U	I	D
G	N	P	R	E	A	P	A	O	H	T	E	O	E	R	U	P	U	U
N	E	D	L	R	R	O	R	E	M	I	N	D	R	E	T	E	N	N
N	A	S	N	N	H	R	R	B	R	E	T	U	R	N	P	S	R	I
E	A	U	N	E	P	E	U	S	E	R	B	T	R	P	N	E	E	H

Pretest

Name _____

Fold the first column under. Take the Pretest and write your answers in the second column. Unfold and self-check your answers. Study the words and write corrections in the third column.

Spelling Words	Take the Pretest	Write Corrections
1. mainly	1.	1.
2. faithful	2.	2.
3. proudly	3.	3.
4. bravely	4.	4.
5. awful	5.	5.
6. lonely	6.	6.
7. friendly	7.	7.
8. careful	8.	8.
9. mouthful	9.	9.
10. thankful	10.	10.
11. nearly	11.	11.
12. slowly	12.	12.
13. handful	13.	13.
14. smoothly	14.	14.
15. cheerful	15.	15.
16. pretty	16.	16.
17. lose	17.	17.
18. control	18.	18.

Challenge Words

19.	19.	19.
20.	20.	20.

➤ The suffix *-ly* added to a word means *characteristic of*.
➤ The suffix *-ful* added to a word means *full of*.

Word Sort

Name _____

Pattern Words Use the key words below to help you sort each pattern word by the indicated pattern.

Pattern Words

mainly	faithful	proudly	bravely	awful
lonely	friendly	careful	mouthful	thankful
nearly	slowly	handful	smoothly	cheerful

Words with -ly — *calmly*

_____ _____

_____ _____

_____ _____

_____ _____

Words with -ful — *fruitful*

_____ _____

_____ _____

_____ _____

_____ _____

Read, Spell, Read!

High Frequency/Tricky Words Read each word out loud. Touch under each letter in each word, spell the word out loud, and read the word again. Then read the sentence. Underline the word in each sentence. Write the answer to the question using the underlined word.

pretty — Elsa wanted the pretty dress she had seen at the mall to wear to school. She was thankful her mom would help her pay for it.
   What did Elsa want?

lose — Mom told Jeff to take care of his new school gear. She did not want him to lose another backpack at school.
   What did Mom not want Jeff to do?

control — Rose had a hard time trying to control her new bike without training wheels. She had to take her time and ride slowly.
   What was hard for Rose to do with her new bike?

Copyright © 2004 by High Noon Books. Permission granted to reproduce for classroom use.

Reading, Writing & Spelling

Name _____

Spelling Words

mainly	faithful	proudly	bravely	awful
lonely	friendly	careful	mouthful	thankful
nearly	slowly	control	smoothly	cheerful

Fill in the Blank
For each line write the word from your spelling list that should fill in the blank.

1. Matt _____ flew our flag outside his tent.
2. We are _____ for good health!
3. He had no _____ over where the game was played?
4. You need to drive _____ past the school.
5. I feel _____ when there is no one to play with me.
6. The team was _____ after they won the game.
7. Pam got sick and felt just _____ all day!
8. The show ran _____ last night.
9. The black car _____ missed hitting the pole.
10. I was very _____ not to get dirty outside.
11. I just met Meg at noon, and she seemed very _____.
12. Tad _____ wants to hear about your trip to France.
13. If someone is _____, it means you can count on them.
14. Pete can't talk with a _____ of yams.

Word Building
Choose a spelling word you did not use above.

15. Which spelling word did you not use above? _____
16. Create new words from the letters of this word and list below:

_____

Word Play

Name _____

Spelling Words

mainly	faithful	proudly	bravely	awful
lonely	friendly	careful	thankful	nearly
pretty	handful	smoothly	cheerful	lose

Exploring Words — Complete the chart. Choose the suffix and add it to the base word to build a word from the spelling list or take the spelling word apart into a base word and suffix.

SAMPLE					
Add the suffix to the base word.	slow	+	ly	=	slowly
Separate base word from suffix.	mouth	+	ful	=	mouthful

1.	main	+		=	
2.		+		=	faithful
3.	friend	+		=	
4.		+		=	thankful
5.		+		=	awful
6.	smooth	+		=	
7.	brave	+		=	
8.	proud	+		=	
9.		+		=	nearly
10.	hand	+		=	
11.		+		=	careful
12.		+		=	cheerful
13.	lone	+		=	

Complete the following **analogies** using spelling words from your list.

1. **Old** is to **new** as **ugly** is to _____.
2. **Quickly** is to **slowly** as **win** is to _____.
3. **Upset** is to **sad** as **happy** is to _____.

Copyright © 2004 by High Noon Books. Permission granted to reproduce for classroom use.

Pretest

Name _____

Fold the first column under. Take the Pretest and write your answers in the second column. Unfold and self-check your answers. Study the words and write corrections in the third column.

Spelling Words	Take the Pretest	Write Corrections
1. careless	1.	1.
2. sickness	2.	2.
3. speechless	3.	3.
4. pointless	4.	4.
5. weakness	5.	5.
6. freshness	6.	6.
7. kindness	7.	7.
8. harmless	8.	8.
9. darkness	9.	9.
10. useless	10.	10.
11. hopeless	11.	11.
12. witness	12.	12.
13. painless	13.	13.
14. likeness	14.	14.
15. goodness	15.	15.
16. carry	16.	16.
17. weird	17.	17.
18. column	18.	18.
Challenge Words 19.	19.	19.
20.	20.	20.

➤ The suffix *-less* added to a word means *without*.
➤ The suffix *-ness* added to a word means *the state of* or *condition of*.

Word Sort

Name _____

Pattern Words Use the key words below to help you sort each pattern word by the indicated pattern.

Pattern Words
careless sickness speechless pointless weakness
freshness kindness harmless darkness useless
hopeless witness painless likeness goodness

Words with -less *fearless*

Words with -ness *meanness*

Read, Spell, Read!

High Frequency/Tricky Words Read each word out loud. Touch under each letter in each word, spell the word out loud, and read the word again. Then read the sentence. Underline the word in each sentence. Write the answer to the question using the underlined word.

carry — Joan's sickness made it hard for her to walk up stairs and carry her bags at the same time. So she asked Meg to come downstairs to help.
What did Joan ask Meg to do?

weird — John saw a weird looking bird at the zoo. It had a long beak and short legs.
How did John think the bird looked?

column — Pat was told to only write in the left column on the spelling page. His teacher said it was pointless to fill in the right column now.
Where does Pat's teacher say to write now?

93

LESSON 22 Reading, Writing & Spelling

Name _____

Spelling Words

careless	sickness	speechless	pointless	weakness	witness
column	freshness	kindness	harmless	darkness	useless
hopeless	painless	likeness	goodness	weird	carry

Clues

Read the clues. Choose the spelling word that best fits the clue.

1. You are this if you can't talk. _____

2. It doesn't hurt. _____

3. It means free from care. _____

4. One who saw something. _____

5. It is the state of being nice. _____

6. It means it is of no good. _____

7. If it has no meaning it is this. _____

8. This is the same as an illness. _____

9. This starts like *well* and ends like *kindness*. _____

10. It means bleak or having no hope. _____

11. It starts like *free* and ends like *likeness*. _____

12. This is the state of being like something. _____

13. This is the state of not being light. _____

14. It means not causing harm. _____

15. It is the state of being good. _____

Each group of words below represents a category.
Find a spelling word that could be grouped with each category and write it on the line provided.

1. haul, lift _____

2. pole, tube _____

3. strange , funny _____

LESSON 22 · Word Play

Name _____

Spelling Words

careless	sickness	speechless	pointless	weakness
freshness	kindness	harmless	darkness	useless
hopeless	witness	painless	likeness	goodness

Crack the Code

Break the code to find your spelling words below.

l ✏	h ☺	less ❄	ness ⌒	are ✳	s ☎	ee 📖	oi ✗	n ✉	r ⌘	ar ☺
f ★	e ⚑	d ♥	o_e 🕐	ai ✈	g 🔒	i ●	ck 💻	p ◆	m ▢	y ↗
c 📂	ch 👍	ea 🔔	k ✋	t 📬	sh ★	u_e ♣	w ⧗	i_e ✂	oo ➹	o ⊕

	Break the code	Make the word
1. ✳ ❄ 📂		
2. ★ ★ ⌒ ⌘ ⚑		
3. ✉ ❄ ◆ ✈		
4. 💻 ⌒ ☎ ●		
5. ✏ ✂ ⌒ ✋		
6. ◆ ☎ 👍 ❄ 📖		
7. ⧗ ⌒ ✋ 🔔		
8. ✗ ◆ ✉ 📬 ❄		
9. ✉ ♥ ● ⌒ ✋		
10. ☎ ♣ ❄		
11. ❄ 🕐 ☺ ◆		
12. ⌒ ⧗ 📬 ●		
13. ☺ ❄ ▢ ☺		
14. ⌒ ☺ ✋ ♥		
15. ↗ 🔒 ⌒ ♥		

Copyright © 2004 by High Noon Books. Permission granted to reproduce for classroom use.

Pretest

Name _____

Fold the first column under. Take the Pretest and write your answers in the second column. Unfold and self-check your answers. Study the words and write corrections in the third column.

Spelling Words	Take the Pretest	Write Corrections
1. bottom	1.	1.
2. kitten	2.	2.
3. pencil	3.	3.
4. funnel	4.	4.
5. happen	5.	5.
6. mitten	6.	6.
7. basket	7.	7.
8. blossom	8.	8.
9. sudden	9.	9.
10. pillow	10.	10.
11. picnic	11.	11.
12. object	12.	12.
13. blanket	13.	13.
14. fabric	14.	14.
15. insist	15.	15.
16. always	16.	16.
17. angle	17.	17.
18. angel	18.	18.
Challenge Words		
19.	19.	19.
20.	20.	20.

➤ Each syllable in a two-syllable word contains a vowel sound. When the first syllable has a short vowel sound, the spelling pattern is often VCCV, with the syllable break between the two consonants. Sometimes the consonants are the same; sometimes they are different.

Word Sort

Name _____

Pattern Words Use the key words below to help you sort each pattern word by the indicated pattern.

Pattern Words

bottom	kitten	pencil	funnel	happen
mitten	basket	blossom	sudden	pillow
picnic	object	blanket	fabric	insist

VCCV Words — helmet	VCCV Words with double consonants — puppet

Read, Spell, Read!

High Frequency/Tricky Words Read each word out loud. Touch under each letter in each word, spell the word out loud, and read the word again. Then read the sentence. Underline the word in each sentence. Write the answer to the question using the underlined word.

always Riding a skateboard was the thing Steve liked to do best.
He knew he needed to always wear the right gear to be safe.
   What did Steve need to do to be safe?

angel The kids hurried to put the bright shiny bulbs on the tree.
The lights shone like stars as Dad placed the angel on top.
   What did Dad put on top of the tree?

angle This week in art class they learned to draw curves and angles.
Becky thought the angles were hard to draw.
   What did Becky think was hard to do in art class?

Reading, Writing & Spelling

Name _____

Spelling Words

bottom	kitten	pencil	funnel	happen
mitten	basket	blossom	sudden	pillow
picnic	object	blanket	fabric	insist

Writing

You just got a baby kitten. How will you take care of it? What will it like to do? Use at least five of your spelling words in your writing below.

_____
_____
_____
_____
_____
_____
_____
_____
_____
_____

Check the following after you have proofread your writing.

- ☐ Check here if you proofread for **misspelled** words.
- ☐ Check here if you proofread for **words** you may have **left out** of your writing.
- ☐ Check here if you proofread for **punctuation**.
- ☐ Check here if you reread your writing to make sure it **makes sense**.

List below the spelling words from your list that you used in your writing.

_____
_____

List other words that were hard to spell. Proofread and check spellings.

_____
_____

Word Play

Name _____

Spelling Words

bottom	kitten	mitten	funnel	happen	pencil
basket	blossom	sudden	pillow	picnic	object
blanket	fabric	insist	always	angle	angel

Crossword

Use the clues provided to fill in the crossword puzzle with your spelling words. Only use each word once.

Across
2. a meal you eat outside
4. a being not from earth
5. part of a plant and may smell sweet
6. you write with this
7. at all times
9. this keeps your hand warm
11. you can carry stuff in this
13. a tube that things flow through
15. not the top
17. a baby cat

Down
1. two lines form this
3. to come to pass
5. used on a bed to keep you warm
8. without warning
10. to be firm
12. you put your head on this
14. same as cloth
16. a thing

Pretest
LESSONS 19-23 REVIEW

Name _____

Fold the first column under. Take the Pretest and write your answers in the second column. Unfold and self-check your answers. Study the words and write corrections in the third column.

Spelling Words	Take the Pretest	Write Corrections
1. unload	1.	1.
2. distract	2.	2.
3. unkept	3.	3.
4. redo	4.	4.
5. disown	5.	5.
6. refill	6.	6.
7. disgust	7.	7.
8. distort	8.	8.
9. unwise	9.	9.
10. recall	10.	10.
11. regroup	11.	11.
12. regard	12.	12.
13. dismiss	13.	13.
14. unlit	14.	14.
15. unfair	15.	15.
16. sure	16.	16.
17. pretty	17.	17.
18. always	18.	18.

Challenge Words

| 19. | 19. | 19. |
| 20. | 20. | 20. |

➤ The prefix *un–* added to a root or base word usually means *not*.
➤ The prefix *dis–* added to a root or base word usually means *not* or *opposite of*.
➤ The prefix *re–* added to a root or base word sometimes means *back* or *again*.

Word Sort — Lessons 19-23 Review

Name _____

Pattern Words   Use the key words below to help you sort each pattern word by the indicated pattern.

Pattern Words

unload	distract	unkept	redo	disown
refill	disgust	distort	unwise	recall
regroup	regard	dismiss	unlit	unfair

Words with un- — untie	Words with dis- — dislike	Words with re- — remake

Read, Spell, Read!

High Frequency/Tricky Words   Read each word out loud. Touch under each letter in each word, spell the word out loud, and read the word again. Then read the sentence. Underline the word in each sentence. Write the answer to the question using the underlined word.

sure   Sam and I joined the chess club and liked to play the game at school. Tim was not sure he knew the rules, so he didn't join the club.
   Why did Tim not join the club?

_____

pretty   The beads on the bride's long white dress caught the light from the sun. Everyone said how pretty she looked on her wedding day.
   How did the bride look?

_____

always   Beth is Jen's best friend. She always knows how to distract her when she's sad and cheer her up.
   Why is Beth Jen's best friend?

_____

Reading, Writing & Spelling
LESSONS 19-23
REVIEW

Name _____

Spelling Words

unload	distract	unkept	redo	disown
refill	disgust	distort	unwise	recall
regroup	regard	dismiss	unlit	unfair

Proofreading — Use proofreading marks to mark the errors in the sentences. Then rewrite the misspelled words with corrections on the lines provided.

Proofreading Marks
∧ Insert   ƛ Delete   ◯ Check Spelling   ≡ Uppercase Needed

The unlit wick did not distrackt from the table setting, and a dim light from the hall cast a gloe into the room. I recal how prette pam looked that night when she met Stan for diner.

List the correct spelling of the misspelled words below.

_____
_____

Mrs Reed did not dismis us on time for lunch again. Everyone felt it was unfare but we also felt it wood be unwize to state this to Mrs. Reed

List the correct spelling of the misspelled words below.

_____
_____

102
Copyright © 2004 by High Noon Books. Permission granted to reproduce for classroom use.

Word Play
LESSONS 19-23
REVIEW

Name _____

Spelling Words

unload	distract	unkept	redo	disown	refill
disgust	distort	unwise	recall	unlit	regard
dismiss	regroup	unfair	sure	always	pretty

Word Paths — Connect one letter from each row to the next to find all the letters in one of your spelling words. Then write the word on the line provided. Each letter should be used once.

D	I	G	G	O	U	T	1. _____
D	I	S	M	I	R	S	2. _____
R	E	S	T	U	S	P	3. _____
D	I	S	R	O	S	T	4. _____

U	N	L	O	T	Y	5. _____
P	E	E	I	T	D	6. _____
U	N	C	T	L		7. _____
R	R	L	A	A	L	8. _____

U	E	W	E	I		9. _____
S	N	R	A		E	10. _____
R	N	F	O			11. _____
U	U	D	I	S	R	12. _____

U	E	W	O	W	S	13. _____
D	N	G	A	P	N	14. _____
A	L	S	E	R	D	15. _____
R	I	K	A	Y	T	16. _____

Pretest

Name _____

Fold the first column under. Take the Pretest and write your answers in the second column. Unfold and self-check your answers. Study the words and write corrections in the third column.

Spelling Words	Take the Pretest	Write Corrections
1. rabbit	1.	1.
2. crazy	2.	2.
3. music	3.	3.
4. pilot	4.	4.
5. event	5.	5.
6. insect	6.	6.
7. apron	7.	7.
8. napkin	8.	8.
9. public	9.	9.
10. problem	10.	10.
11. chosen	11.	11.
12. human	12.	12.
13. depend	13.	13.
14. hotel	14.	14.
15. behind	15.	15.
16. upon	16.	16.
17. reign	17.	17.
18. genius	18.	18.
Challenge Words		
19.	19.	19.
20.	20.	20.

➤ Each syllable in a two-syllable word contains a vowel sound. When the first syllable has a short vowel sound, the spelling pattern is often VCCV, with the syllable break between the two consonants. Sometimes the consonants are the same; sometimes they are different.

➤ When the first syllable has a long vowel sound, the spelling pattern is usually VCV, with the syllable break after the first vowel making the first syllable open.

104

Copyright © 2004 by High Noon Books. Permission granted to reproduce for classroom use.

Word Sort

Name _____

Pattern Words Use the key words below to help you sort each pattern word by the indicated pattern.

Pattern Words

rabbit	crazy	music	pilot	event
insect	apron	napkin	public	problem
chosen	human	depend	hotel	behind

VCCV Words — picnic

VCV Words — paper

Read, Spell, Read!

High Frequency/Tricky Words Read each word out loud. Touch under each letter in each word, spell the word out loud, and read the word again. Then read the sentence. Underline the word in each sentence. Write the answer to the question using the underlined word.

upon The teacher told the class that fairytales often start with "Once upon a time" and poems only sometimes have words that rhyme.
What did the teacher say fairytales start with?

reign It seemed like a long time to rule, but the king's reign lasted for only ten years. Everyone wondered who would be the next ruler.
What lasted for ten years?

genius Everyone called the math teacher a genius. She seemed to know everything and was very smart!
What did they call the math teacher?

Copyright © 2004 by High Noon Books. Permission granted to reproduce for classroom use.

LESSON 25 Reading, Writing & Spelling

Name _____

Spelling Words

rabbit	crazy	music	pilot	event
insect	apron	napkin	public	problem
chosen	human	depend	hotel	behind

Dictionary & Vocabulary Connections

pilot (pī•lət) n. **1.** One who flies a plane: *The pilot flew to France. adj.* **2.** A kind of light in a stove: *The pilot light in the stove went out.* n. **3.** A new T.V. show: *Lots of people watched the pilot for the new game show.*

1. Using the information above, what part or parts of speech is the word *pilot?*

   _____

2. Using all definitions above, create a web of synonyms for *pilot.*
   You can use words or phrases.

   _____   (pilot)   _____

   _____   _____

3. Which of the following could be the guide words for *pilot?* _____
   a. pillow   pinch   b. pinch   pink   c. pipe   pinch

4. Use definition #1 above and write your own sentence using the
   word *pilot.*   _____

   _____

5. Use definition #3 above and write your own sentence using the
   word *pilot.*   _____

   _____

6. List up to three words from the spelling list that come before and after
   pilot in the dictionary.

   Before   After

   _____   _____

   _____   _____

   _____   _____

Word Play

Name _____

Spelling Words

rabbit	crazy	music	pilot	event	insect
apron	napkin	public	problem	chosen	human
depend	hotel	behind	upon	reign	genius

Word Find

Find the spelling words in the word find puzzle below. Circle each word.

B	T	E	P	S	D	N	T	P	D	P	C	E	M	E	B	U	P	U
E	E	C	T	H	I	V	I	N	B	E	E	V	E	N	T	C	H	R
E	A	O	E	K	T	N	M	O	P	L	P	Z	I	E	B	U	N	N
H	E	C	P	S	L	P	G	P	P	E	E	E	L	L	G	S	I	U
C	I	A	S	L	N	E	U	U	T	P	E	U	N	A	E	O	P	R
A	N	U	R	C	O	I	T	B	M	H	B	U	P	D	N	U	N	E
I	B	B	E	H	I	N	D	O	L	I	I	M	U	S	I	C	E	N
P	R	O	B	L	E	M	E	D	H	I	L	E	E	N	U	T	S	P
U	O	N	R	N	P	O	T	N	T	U	C	O	E	N	S	O	O	U
P	B	R	P	I	L	O	T	I	E	I	N	T	S	P	N	H	H	L
L	D	L	E	N	I	P	P	D	B	A	P	R	O	N	L	U	C	N
B	K	M	E	I	H	R	E	M	O	B	Z	T	K	U	C	M	B	T
S	C	N	S	T	G	P	E	E	U	H	A	I	N	K	L	A	I	E
P	P	L	M	O	T	N	O	E	C	P	B	R	E	E	H	N	D	C
I	A	H	C	R	A	Z	Y	O	A	R	I	H	E	N	N	U	L	E
A	P	I	I	I	P	O	E	N	M	R	S	S	A	S	T	E	L	I

Copyright © 2004 by High Noon Books. Permission granted to reproduce for classroom use.

Pretest

Name _____

Fold the first column under. Take the Pretest and write your answers in the second column. Unfold and self-check your answers. Study the words and write corrections in the third column.

Spelling Words	Take the Pretest	Write Corrections
1. finish	1.	1.
2. planet	2.	2.
3. shadow	3.	3.
4. lady	4.	4.
5. punish	5.	5.
6. habit	6.	6.
7. begin	7.	7.
8. silent	8.	8.
9. cabin	9.	9.
10. basic	10.	10.
11. prison	11.	11.
12. event	12.	12.
13. salad	13.	13.
14. depend	14.	14.
15. pupil	15.	15.
16. about	16.	16.
17. human	17.	17.
18. pigeon	18.	18.
Challenge Words		
19.	19.	19.
20.	20.	20.

➤ Each syllable in a two-syllable word contains a vowel sound. When the first syllable of a VCV word has a short sound, the syllable breaks before the second vowel making the first syllable closed.

108

Copyright © 2004 by High Noon Books. Permission granted to reproduce for classroom use.

Word Sort

Name _____

Pattern Words Use the key words below to help you sort each pattern word by the indicated pattern.

Pattern Words

finish	planet	shadow	lady	punish
habit	begin	silent	cabin	basic
prison	event	salad	depend	pupil

VC / V Words   edit

V / CV Words   open

Read, Spell, Read!

High Frequency/Tricky Words Read each word out loud. Touch under each letter in each word, spell the word out loud, and read the word again. Then read the sentence. Underline the word in each sentence. Write the answer to the question using the underlined word.

about — You have to be at least four feet tall to go on the ride. Max is only about three feet tall and can't ride this time.
How tall is Max?

human — Pam's teacher said human beings cannot live on Mars. Pam thinks maybe someday they will.
Who can't live on Mars?

pigeon — As Amy was playing in the park, she saw a pigeon land on the fence. Amy tried to be silent to get a closer look.
What did Amy see land on the fence?

109

Copyright © 2004 by High Noon Books. Permission granted to reproduce for classroom use.

LESSON 26 · Reading, Writing & Spelling

Name _____

Spelling Words

finish	planet	shadow	lady	punish
habit	begin	silent	cabin	basic
prison	event	salad	depend	pupil

Writing

You could travel in a spaceship. Where would you go? What would you do? Use at least five of your spelling words in your writing below.

_____

_____

_____

_____

_____

_____

_____

_____

_____

_____

_____

Check the following after you have proofread your writing.

☐ Check here if you proofread for **misspelled** words.
☐ Check here if you proofread for **words** you may have **left out** of your writing.
☐ Check here if you proofread for **punctuation**.
☐ Check here if you reread your writing to make sure it **makes sense**.

List below the spelling words from your list that you used in your writing.

_____

_____

List other words that were hard to spell. Proofread and check spellings.

_____

_____

110 Copyright © 2004 by High Noon Books. Permission granted to reproduce for classroom use.

Word Play

Name _____

Spelling Words

finish	planet	shadow	lady	punish	habit
begin	silent	cabin	basic	prison	event
salad	depend	pupil	about	pigeon	human

Crossword — Use the clues provided to fill in the crossword puzzle with your spelling words. Only use each word once.

Down
1. a dark outline
2. a person
4. not fancy
6. to place trust in
7. to start
8. what happens when you are at fault
9. to be done with
10. a child in class
16. something that happens
18. a woman

Across
3. almost
5. a dish of leafy green food
11. a bird
12. a small house
13. a jail
14. something you do over and over
15. no noise
17. one of nine large bodies in the sky

Pretest

Name _____

Fold the first column under. Take the Pretest and write your answers in the second column. Unfold and self-check your answers. Study the words and write corrections in the third column.

Spelling Words	Take the Pretest	Write Corrections
1. became	1.	1.
2. decide	2.	2.
3. polite	3.	3.
4. reptile	4.	4.
5. costume	5.	5.
6. behave	6.	6.
7. unsafe	7.	7.
8. exhale	8.	8.
9. combine	9.	9.
10. athlete	10.	10.
11. female	11.	11.
12. advice	12.	12.
13. volume	13.	13.
14. locate	14.	14.
15. suppose	15.	15.
16. any	16.	16.
17. rhythm	17.	17.
18. rhyme	18.	18.

Challenge Words

19.	19.	19.
20.	20.	20.

➤ When the second syllable of a two-syllable word has a long vowel sound, sometimes the word ends in a silent-e.

112

Word Sort

Name _____

Pattern Words Use the key words below to help you sort each pattern word by the indicated pattern.

Pattern Words

became	decide	polite	reptile	costume
behave	unsafe	exhale	combine	athlete
female	advice	volume	locate	suppose

Open syllable + silent e syllable — *pirate*

Closed syllable + silent e syllable — *manage*

Read, Spell, Read!

High Frequency/Tricky Words Read each word out loud. Touch under each letter in each word, spell the word out loud, and read the word again. Then read the sentence. Underline the word in each sentence. Write the answer to the question using the underlined word.

any — Mom needed some flour to bake bread. There was none in the pantry. She called her friend to ask, "Do you have any flour?"
What did Mom ask her friend?

rhythm — Matt had just learned to play the drums. He was having a hard time hearing the rhythm of the song at his lesson.
What was Matt having a hard time with at his lesson?

rhyme — Jill can tell you when two words rhyme, but she cannot tell when two words start with the same sound. Her teacher is helping her learn.
What can Jill tell you?

113

Name _____

Spelling Words

became	decide	polite	reptile	costume
behave	unsafe	exhale	combine	athlete
female	advice	volume	locate	suppose

Proofreading — Use proofreading marks to mark the errors in the sentences. Then rewrite the sentences with the corrections on the lines provided.

Proofreading Marks

∧ Insert   ⋎ Delete   ◯ Check Spelling   ≡ Uppercase Needed

The female athlet could not complet at the meat. It would have been unsaffe do to her sprained wrist they could not find any of the other girls to replase her.

List the correct spelling of the misspelled words below.

———————————————————————

Ross trid to locat the costum he wanted to where for the party. It was supose to be in the attic but he couldn't find it. Tad gave him some good advise and told him to look again in the morning when it wouldn't be so dark

List the correct spelling of the misspelled words below.

114   Copyright © 2004 by High Noon Books. Permission granted to reproduce for classroom use.

Name _____

Spelling Words

became	decide	polite	reptile	costume	behave
unsafe	exhale	combine	athlete	female	advice
volume	locate	suppose	any	rhythm	rhyme

Word Find

Find the spelling words in the word find puzzle below. Circle each word.

L	T	E	A	E	P	E	M	O	H	E	M	E	I	E	C	E	F	V
E	U	N	S	A	F	E	T	A	I	T	E	D	N	F	M	A	C	F
A	L	U	S	M	B	E	E	S	L	V	E	I	S	A	L	A	P	E
T	N	A	D	N	C	E	E	A	A	E	E	C	M	T	U	O	L	O
E	E	I	H	E	D	A	U	H	D	E	S	E	I	E	L	B	E	T
E	A	E	T	X	E	Y	E	D	M	T	O	D	A	I	A	E	T	R
R	T	E	C	B	E	B	A	T	E	B	P	C	T	E	E	C	E	L
C	E	Y	U	O	E	B	D	M	E	P	E	L	C	E	B	L	V
L	D	P	N	E	Y	C	U	F	M	T	U	O	O	O	O	E	S	H	M
B	V	L	T	A	A	L	A	U	Y	B	S	B	C	S	M	P	T	O
M	E	E	H	I	O	O	S	M	Y	U	I	O	A	T	Y	E	A	D
A	A	L	I	V	L	Y	M	E	E	D	E	N	T	U	E	O	E	C
V	A	B	E	N	M	E	N	H	R	H	Y	M	E	M	X	I	Y	F
E	A	E	R	H	Y	T	H	M	F	E	M	A	L	E	E	A	L	L
A	D	V	I	C	E	I	U	A	H	E	C	O	M	B	I	N	E	N
E	F	I	H	I	R	Y	I	I	X	E	C	P	C	D	L	M	L	R

Copyright © 2004 by High Noon Books. Permission granted to reproduce for classroom use.

115

Pretest

Name _____

Fold the first column under. Take the Pretest and write your answers in the second column. Unfold and self-check your answers. Study the words and write corrections in the third column.

Spelling Words	Take the Pretest	Write Corrections
1. enter	1.	1.
2. over	2.	2.
3. under	3.	3.
4. flutter	4.	4.
5. river	5.	5.
6. shelter	6.	6.
7. vapor	7.	7.
8. after	8.	8.
9. winter	9.	9.
10. voter	10.	10.
11. lever	11.	11.
12. acorn	12.	12.
13. sister	13.	13.
14. motor	14.	14.
15. driver	15.	15.
16. today	16.	16.
17. quizzes	17.	17.
18. recipe	18.	18.

Challenge Words

19.	19.	19.
20.	20.	20.

➤ Each syllable in a two-syllable word contains a vowel sound. When the first syllable has a short vowel sound, the spelling pattern is often VCCV, with the syllable break between the two consonants making the first syllable closed.

➤ Sometimes the spelling pattern is VCV. When the syllable breaks before the second vowel, the first syllable has a short vowel sound and is closed. When the syllable breaks after the first vowel, the first syllable has a long vowel sound and is open.

Word Sort

Name _____

Pattern Words Use the key words below to help you sort each pattern word by the indicated pattern.

Pattern Words

enter	over	under	flutter	river
shelter	vapor	after	winter	voter
lever	acorn	sister	motor	driver

VC/CV with r-controlled *shelter*	V/CV with r-controlled *voter*	VC/V with r-controlled *never*

Read, Spell, Read!

High Frequency/Tricky Words Read each word out loud. Touch under each letter in each word, spell the word out loud, and read the word again. Then read the sentence. Underline the word in each sentence. Write the answer to the question using the underlined word.

today — Mrs. Capps said we would do our play in class today but there was no time. Maybe we can do it after school.
When did Mrs. Capps say the play would happen?

quizzes — Alex took two quizzes this week at school. He was proud that he did well on both of them.
What was Alex proud of this week?

recipe — Kim's soup tasted so good! Jill asked for the recipe.
What did Jill ask Kim for?

LESSON 28
Reading, Writing & Spelling

Name _____

Spelling Words

enter	over	under	flutter	river
shelter	vapor	after	winter	voter
lever	acorn	sister	motor	driver

Dictionary & Vocabulary Connections

shelter (shel•ter) *n.* **1.** Something that gives cover from the weather: *The cave made a good shelter.* *v.* **2.** To protect or provide cover: *Will the trees shelter us?*

1. Using the information above, what part or parts of speech is the word *shelter?* _____

2. Using both definitions above, create a web of synonyms for *shelter*. You can use words or phrases.

   _____   shelter   _____

   _____   _____

3. Which of the following could be the guide words for *shelter?*
   a. shelve   shift   b. sheer   shelve   c. shell   shelf

4. Use definition #1 above and write your own sentence using the word *shelter*. _____

   _____

5. Use definition #3 above and write your own sentence using the word *shelter*. _____

   _____

6. List up to three words from the spelling list that come before and after *shelter* in the dictionary.

   Before   After

   _____   _____

   _____   _____

   _____   _____

118   Copyright © 2004 by High Noon Books. Permission granted to reproduce for classroom use.

LESSON 28 · Word Play

Name _____

Spelling Words

enter	over	under	flutter	river	shelter
vapor	after	winter	voter	lever	acorn
sister	motor	driver	today	quizzes	recipe

Exploring Words

Complete the chart. Before adding *the ending* to the base word to build a word from the spelling list, determine if you need to *drop the e, double the final consonant*, add *s* to make it plural, or add *es* to make it plural.

SAMPLE

	Closed	Open		R-controlled		
Fill in the closed syllable and the r-controlled syllable to form the word.	flut		+	ter	=	flutter
Fill in the r-controlled syllable and the word.		a	+	corn	=	acorn
Fill in the open syllable and the word.		vo	+	ter	=	voter

	Closed	Open		R-controlled		
1.			+		=	shelter
2.		o	+		=	
3.			+	ver	=	
4.	en		+		=	
5.			+	por	=	
6.	af		+		=	
7.	win		+		=	
8.		mo	+		=	
9.	sis		+		=	
10.			+		=	river
11.	un		+		=	

Complete the following **analogies** using spelling words from your list.

1. **Play** is to **script** as **food** is to _____.

2. **Moon** is to **sun** as **tonight** is to _____.

3. **Peach** is to **peaches** as **quiz** is to _____.

Copyright © 2004 by High Noon Books. Permission granted to reproduce for classroom use

Name _____

Fold the first column under. Take the Pretest and write your answers in the second column. Unfold and self-check your answers. Study the words and write corrections in the third column.

Spelling Words	Take the Pretest	Write Corrections
1. recline	1.	1.
2. unlock	2.	2.
3. restock	3.	3.
4. replant	4.	4.
5. refresh	5.	5.
6. untwist	6.	6.
7. discuss	7.	7.
8. uncap	8.	8.
9. unused	9.	9.
10. distaste	10.	10.
11. unsent	11.	11.
12. reface	12.	12.
13. rerun	13.	13.
14. reflex	14.	14.
15. unmet	15.	15.
16. never	16.	16.
17. distinct	17.	17.
18. license	18.	18.

Challenge Words
19.
20.

➤ The prefix *un-* added to a root or base word means *not*.
➤ The prefix *dis-* added to a root or base word means *not* or *opposite of*.
➤ The prefix *re-* added to a root or base word sometimes means *back* or *again*.

Name _____

Pattern Words Use the key words below to help you sort each pattern word by the indicated pattern.

Pattern Words				
recline	unlock	restock	replant	refresh
untwist	discuss	uncap	unused	distaste
unsent	reface	rerun	reflex	unmet

Words with *re-* `redo`   Words with *dis-* `distrust`   Words with *un-* `uncap`

Read, Spell, Read!

High Frequency/Tricky Words Read each word out loud. Touch under each letter in each word, spell the word out loud, and read the word again. Then read the sentence. Underline the word in each sentence. Write the answer to the question using the underlined word.

never   Jorge said he would never go to Maine again. It was too cold for his taste.
   What did Jorge say about his trip to Maine?

distinct   A distinct smell was coming from the barn. Pam was sure a skunk had sprayed the wood pile inside.
   What was strange about the barn?

license   The license plate was missing from Kim's car. She was lucky she did not get a ticket!
   Why could Kim have gotten a ticket?

Lesson 29 — Reading, Writing & Spelling

Name _____

Spelling Words

recline	unlock	restock	replant	refresh
untwist	discuss	uncap	unused	distaste
unsent	reface	rerun	reflex	unmet

Fill in the Blank
For each line write the word from your spelling list that should fill in the blank.

1. The clerk planned to _____ the store shelves.
2. Phil had to _____ the grass each Spring.
3. Please _____ the juice for me.
4. I saw a _____ of the show last night.
5. The bike they bought was _____.
6. Her blink was a _____ to the bright light.
7. Sam has a _____ for fruit.
8. The box is still on the shelf _____.
9. Her sales goals were _____ for the year.
10. The chair will _____ if you push back on it.
11. A glass of water will _____ me.
12. I would like to _____ a new job with you.
13. _____ the door so I can come in.
14. Steve wants to _____ the kitchen doors.

Word Building
Choose a spelling word you did not use above.

15. Which spelling word did you not use above? _____

16. Create new words from the letters of this word and list below:

_____

122

Copyright © 2004 by High Noon Books. Permission granted to reproduce for classroom use.

LESSON 29 · Word Play

Name _____

Spelling Words

recline	unlock	restock	replant	refresh
untwist	discuss	unused	distaste	unsent
reflex	never	distinct	license	unmet

Crack the Code

Break the code to find your spelling words below.

m ✐	dis ☺	re ❄	un 〰	n ☼	d ☎	l 📖	b ✗	a ✉	r ⌘
i ★	u ⚑	a_e ♥	v 🕐	ed ✈	u_e 🔒	i_e 💧	s 💻	p ◆	c ✂
o 📁	ck 👍	f 🔔	sh ✋	w 📫	ss ★(circle)	x ♣	er ⧗	t 😐	e ➶

	Break the code	Make the word
1. ◆ ❄ ☼ 😐 📖 ✉		
2. ✂ ❄ 📖 ☼ 💧		
3. 💻 ☺ ♥ 😐 😐		
4. 💻 ☼ 〰 😐 ➶		
5. ⧗ ☼ 🕐 ➶		
6. 👍 📖 〰 📁		
7. 😐 😐 ✂ ★ ☺ ☼		
8. 🔔 ❄ ➶ ⌘ ✋		
9. ❄ 😐 💻 👍 📁		
10. 〰 ✈ 🔒 💻		
11. 〰 😐 😐 ★ 💻 📫		
12. ❄ ♣ ➶ 🔔 📖		
13. ★(circle) ☺ ⚑ ✂		
14. ✂ ➶ ☼ 💻 📖 ★ ➶		
15. ➶ 😐 〰 ✐		

Copyright © 2004 by High Noon Books. Permission granted to reproduce for classroom use.

Pretest
LESSONS 25-29
REVIEW

Name _____

Fold the first column under. Take the Pretest and write your answers in the second column. Unfold and self-check your answers. Study the words and write corrections in the third column.

Spelling Words	Take the Pretest	Write Corrections
1. plenty	1.	1.
2. item	2.	2.
3. puppet	3.	3.
4. budget	4.	4.
5. credit	5.	5.
6. protect	6.	6.
7. second	7.	7.
8. wages	8.	8.
9. wisdom	9.	9.
10. adjust	10.	10.
11. basic	11.	11.
12. sofa	12.	12.
13. helmet	13.	13.
14. cactus	14.	14.
15. solid	15.	15.
16. any	16.	16.
17. today	17.	17.
18. never	18.	18.

Challenge Words

19.	19.	19.
20.	20.	20.

➤ Each syllable in a two-syllable word contains a vowel sound. When the first syllable has a short vowel sound, the spelling pattern is often VCCV, with the syllable break between the two consonants making the first syllable closed.

➤ Sometimes the spelling pattern is VCV. When the syllable breaks before the second vowel, the first syllable has a short vowel sound and is closed. When the syllable breaks after the first vowel, the first syllable has a long vowel sound and is open.

Copyright © 2004 by High Noon Books. Permission granted to reproduce for classroom use.

Word Sort
LESSONS 25-29 REVIEW

Name _____

Pattern Words Use the key words below to help you sort each pattern word by the indicated pattern.

Pattern Words				
plenty	item	puppet	budget	credit
protect	second	wages	wisdom	adjust
basic	sofa	helmet	cactus	solid

VC / CV Words — canyon	V / CV Words — open	VC / V Words — panel
_____	_____	_____
_____	_____	_____
_____	_____	_____
_____	_____	_____

Read, Spell, Read!

High Frequency/Tricky Words Read each word out loud. Touch under each letter in each word, spell the word out loud, and read the word again. Then read the sentence. Underline the word in each sentence. Write the answer to the question using the underlined word.

any — Jason ran to Chad's house to trade baseball cards. Jason was sad to learn that Chad did not have any cards left. He had given them away.
 Why was Jason sad?

today — Matt will get his first chance to pitch at the game today. His mom and dad will come to watch.
 When will Matt get his chance to pitch?

never — Vasya said he would never join the tennis team. Basketball is his best sport, and he does not have time to do both!
 What did Vasya say about joining the tennis team?

Copyright © 2004 by High Noon Books. Permission granted to reproduce for classroom use.

125

Name _____

Spelling Words

plenty	item	puppet	budget	credit
protect	second	wages	wisdom	adjust
basic	sofa	helmet	cactus	solid

Clues

Read the clues. Choose the spelling word that best fits the clue.

1. You can play with this on your hand. _____
2. It means lots of. _____
3. This is a money plan. _____
4. This means plain. _____
5. It's a thing that can be bought. _____
6. This is the same as a couch. _____
7. This means to change so as to make it fit. _____
8. It means to know what is right. _____
9. This word starts like *crush* and ends like *bit*. _____
10. You get paid this when you do a job. _____
11. You wear this when you ride a bike. _____
12. This is a spiny plant. _____
13. It does not have any holes in it. _____
14. This is to keep from harm. _____
15. It means you are after first. _____

Each group of words below represents a category.
Find a spelling word that could be grouped with each category and write it on the line provided.

1. chair, bench _____
2. rose, hedge _____
3. doll, block _____

Word Play
LESSONS 25-29
REVIEW

Name _____

Spelling Words

plenty	item	puppet	budget	credit	protect
second	wages	wisdom	adjust	basic	sofa
helmet	cactus	solid	any	today	never

Word Paths — Connect one letter from each row to the next to find all the letters in one of your spelling words. Then write the word on the line provided. Each letter should be used once.

W	I	G	I	O	
S	A	S	D	D	M
W	O	F	E	S	
S	O	L	A		

1. _____
2. _____
3. _____
4. _____

A	L	J	M	Y	
T	D	D	A		T
I	T	E	U	T	
P	O	E	N	S	Y

5. _____
6. _____
7. _____
8. _____

P	R	O	T	E	T	T
P	U	C	P	U	S	
C	A	P	T	E	T	
C	R	E	D	I	C	

9. _____
10. _____
11. _____
12. _____

B	E	Y		E	
N	U	L	E	R	T
A	E	D	M		
H	N	V	G	E	T

13. _____
14. _____
15. _____
16. _____

Copyright © 2004 by High Noon Books. Permission granted to reproduce for classroom use.

Name _____

Fold the first column under. Take the Pretest and write your answers in the second column. Unfold and self-check your answers. Study the words and write corrections in the third column.

Spelling Words	Take the Pretest	Write Corrections
1. involve	1.	1.
2. impede	2.	2.
3. immune	3.	3.
4. insult	4.	4.
5. import	5.	5.
6. infect	6.	6.
7. impulse	7.	7.
8. inept	8.	8.
9. improve	9.	9.
10. infest	10.	10.
11. impress	11.	11.
12. intense	12.	12.
13. impale	13.	13.
14. inspect	14.	14.
15. imprint	15.	15.
16. around	16.	16.
17. aspirin	17.	17.
18. interest	18.	18.

Challenge Words

19.	19.	19.
20.	20.	20.

➤ The prefix *im–* or *in–* added to a root or base word means *not*.

Word Sort

Name _____

Pattern Words Use the key words below to help you sort each pattern word by the indicated pattern.

Pattern Words				
involve	impede	immune	insult	import
infect	impulse	inept	improve	infest
impress	intense	impale	inspect	imprint

Words with im- — imprint

Words with in- — infest

Read, Spell, Read!

High Frequency/Tricky Words Read each word out loud. Touch under each letter in each word, spell the word out loud, and read the word again. Then read the sentence. Underline the word in each sentence. Write the answer to the question using the underlined word.

around The music played a sweet tune as Erin went around and around on the merry-go-round. This was the best part about the visit to the park!
What did Jane like best about the park?

aspirin Jack found the first aide kit under the seat of the car.
Thank goodness there was still one packet of aspirin left!
What did Jack want from the first aide kit?

interest Dwight had a real interest in making the swimming team.
He asked his dad to get him swimming lessons for his birthday.
Why did Dwight want swimming lessons?

129

LESSON 31 Reading, Writing & Spelling

Name _____

Spelling Words

involve	immune	insult	import	impulse
inept	improve	infest	intense	impale
inspect	imprint	around	aspirin	interest

Fill in the Blank

For each line write the word from your spelling list that should fill in the blank.

1. She thinks she is _____ to getting a cold.

2. The fireman came to _____ our classroom for safety.

3. Maria was glad she had a chance to _____ her test score.

4. Becky had an _____ in learning to sew.

5. Ray was worried that fleas would _____ his home.

6. Jay is _____ at cooking.

7. We _____ bananas from South America.

8. Meg had an _____ to buy ice cream.

9. Joan played an _____ game of softball.

10. His plans did not _____ me.

11. Be careful! The pencil could _____ you.

12. Rich did not _____ Sam even though he was rude to him.

13. She took some _____ to help her headache.

14. Jeff ran _____ the track.

Word Building

Choose a spelling word you did not use above.

15. Which spelling word did you not use above? _____

16. Create new words from the letters of this word and list below:

_____

130   Copyright © 2004 by High Noon Books. Permission granted to reproduce for classroom use.

Word Play

Name _____

Spelling Words

involve	impede	immune	insult	import
infect	impulse	inept	improve	infest
impress	intense	interest	inspect	imprint

Exploring Words — Complete the chart. Choose letters or letter pairs to build a word from the spelling list. Or, fill in the missing parts of completed words.

SAMPLE					
Build the word.	in	+	fect	=	infect

1.		+		=	involve
2.		+		=	impulse
3.	im	+	print	=	
4.		+		=	impede
5.		+		=	insult
6.		+		=	inept
7.	in	+	spect	=	
8.		+		=	improve
9.		+		=	impress
10.		+		=	infest
11.	im	+	port	=	
12.		+		=	intense

Complete the following **analogies** using spelling words from your list.

1. **Night** is to **day** as **export** is to _____.
2. **Sunburn** is to **sunscreen** as **sick** is to _____.
3. **Glad** is to **happy** as **hobby** is to _____.

131

Name _____

Fold the first column under. Take the Pretest and write your answers in the second column. Unfold and self-check your answers. Study the words and write corrections in the third column.

Spelling Words	Take the Pretest	Write Corrections
1. misuse	1.	1.
2. mistake	2.	2.
3. pretend	3.	3.
4. mistrust	4.	4.
5. prefer	5.	5.
6. misspell	6.	6.
7. prebake	7.	7.
8. misdial	8.	8.
9. mislead	9.	9.
10. precut	10.	10.
11. prepaid	11.	11.
12. misprint	12.	12.
13. preheat	13.	13.
14. misjudge	14.	14.
15. mismatch	15.	15.
16. because	16.	16.
17. symbol	17.	17.
18. thorough	18.	18.

Challenge Words

| 19. | 19. | 19. |
| 20. | 20. | 20. |

➤ The prefix *pre-* added to a root or base word means *before*.
➤ The prefix *mis-* added to a root or base word means *wrongly*.

132

Copyright © 2004 by High Noon Books. Permission granted to reproduce for classroom use.

Word Sort

Name _____

Pattern Words Use the key words below to help you sort each pattern word by the indicated pattern.

Pattern Words
misuse mistake pretend mistrust prefer
misspell prebake misdial mislead precut
prepaid misprint preheat misjudge mismatch

Words with *mis-* *misfit*	Words with *pre-* *preteach*
_____ _____	_____ _____
_____ _____	_____ _____
_____ _____	_____ _____
_____ _____	_____ _____

Read, Spell, Read!

High Frequency/Tricky Words Read each word out loud. Touch under each letter in each word, spell the word out loud, and read the word again. Then read the sentence. Underline the word in each sentence. Write the answer to the question using the underlined word.

because The team went to get ice cream after school today because they heard there was a sale. Cones and shakes were half price!
Why did the team decide to get ice cream today?

_____

symbol Sonlay did not know the skull and cross bone symbol for poison. His mom had to explain the label to him.
What did Sonlay's mom have to explain?

_____

thorough Ann was very thorough when she cleaned Sam's house. Not a speck of dust could be found anywhere!
How well did Ann clean Sam's house?

_____

Copyright © 2004 by High Noon Books. Permission granted to reproduce for classroom use.

Spelling Words

misuse	mistake	pretend	mistrust	prefer
misspell	prebake	misdial	mislead	precut
prepaid	misprint	symbol	misjudge	mismatch

Clues
Read the clues. Choose the spelling word that best fits the clue.

1. This is to make believe. _____
2. Choosing one thing over another. _____
3. This is when you do something wrong. _____
4. This means to cook before. _____
5. You did this if you paid early. _____
6. It means to judge wrongly. _____
7. When something is cut before it is used. _____
8. It means to lead in the wrong way. _____
9. It means to not spell words right. _____
10. It means to dial wrong. _____
11. It is a sign used to show something. _____
12. This is a wrong match. _____
13. This means to not treat right. _____
14. This starts like *mistake* and ends like *rent*. _____
15. This means lack of trust. _____

Each group of words below represents a category.
Find a spelling word that could be grouped with each category and write it on the line provided.

1. broil, preheat _____
2. trusted, trusting _____
3. heart, plus sign _____

LESSON 32 · Word Play

Name _____

Spelling Words

misuse	mistake	pretend	mistrust	prefer
misspell	prebake	misdial	mislead	prepaid
preheat	misjudge	mismatch	thorough	because

Crack the Code

Break the code to find your spelling words below.

Code key:
- th ✏️
- au ☺
- h ❄️
- mis 👓
- pre ☼
- u_e ☎️
- t 📖
- e ✉️
- k ⌘
- u ⌘
- p ☺
- f ★
- ll 🏴
- i ♥
- l ⏰
- a ✈️
- or 🔒
- j 💧
- n 💻
- b ◆
- s ✂️
- y ⊕
- r 📂
- a_e 👍
- er 🔔
- ea ✋
- d 📬
- c ★(star)
- ai ♣
- dge ⏳
- tch ☐
- ough 🚀
- m ✠

	Break the code	Make the word
1. ✉️ ◆ 👍 ☼		
2. ❄️ ☼ 📖 ✋		
3. ☎️ 👓 ✂️		
4. ✉️ 📖 👍 👓		
5. 🚀 🔒 ✏️		
6. ⌘ ⏳ 👓 💧		
7. 👓 📂 ✂️ 📖 📖 ⌘		
8. ✗ 📖 💻 ☼ 📬		
9. ✈️ 📬 ⏰ 👓 ♥		
10. ⏰ 📬 👓 ✋		
11. ★ ☼ 🔔		
12. ☺ ◆ ✗ ✗ ★ ✂️		
13. 👓 ✂️ 🏴 ☺ ✗		
14. 👓 ☐ ✈️ 🚀		
15. ♣ ☺ 📬 ☼		

Copyright © 2004 by High Noon Books. Permission granted to reproduce for classroom use.

Name _____

Fold the first column under. Take the Pretest and write your answers in the second column. Unfold and self-check your answers. Study the words and write corrections in the third column.

Spelling Words	Take the Pretest	Write Corrections
1. delete	1.	1.
2. defend	2.	2.
3. preset	3.	3.
4. defeat	4.	4.
5. deplete	5.	5.
6. delay	6.	6.
7. prerinse	7.	7.
8. decline	8.	8.
9. deform	9.	9.
10. preplan	10.	10.
11. decode	11.	11.
12. prevent	12.	12.
13. precede	13.	13.
14. prelaunch	14.	14.
15. preflight	15.	15.
16. again	16.	16.
17. bargain	17.	17.
18. certain	18.	18.

Challenge Words

19.	19.	19.
20.	20.	20.

➤ The prefix *de-* added to a root or base word means *opposite*.
➤ The prefix *pre-* added to a root or base word means *before*.

136

Word Sort

Pattern Words Use the key words below to help you sort each pattern word by the indicated pattern.

Pattern Words				
delete	defend	preset	defeat	deplete
delay	prerinse	decline	deform	preplan
decode	prevent	precede	prelaunch	preflight

Words with de- — deface

Words with pre- — precook

Read, Spell, Read!

High Frequency/Tricky Words Read each word out loud. Touch under each letter in each word, spell the word out loud, and read the word again. Then read the sentence. Underline the word in each sentence. Write the answer to the question using the underlined word.

again — It was clear the snow would soon be gone. Pat did not want to wait until next year to use his new snowboard again!
What did Pat not want to wait to do?

bargain — Erin was shopping at the new store downtown. She was thrilled to find a skirt on sale that was a true bargain.
What was Erin thrilled about?

certain — Yuri told his mom he was certain he would get all A's on his report card. He had studied very hard for the past few months.
What did Yuri tell his mom about his report card?

Copyright © 2004 by High Noon Books. Permission granted to reproduce for classroom use.

Reading, Writing & Spelling

Name _____

Spelling Words

delete	defend	preset	defeat	deplete
delay	prerinse	decline	deform	preplan
decode	prevent	precede	prelaunch	preflight

Proofreading — Use proofreading marks to mark the errors in the sentences. Then rewrite the misspelled words with corrections on the lines provided.

Proofreading Marks
∧ Insert   ℓ Delete   ◯ Check Spelling   ≡ Uppercase Needed

As we boarded the plane the pilote gave us some preflite news. Their would be a short ten-minute dalay while they cleared the runway. The alarm on my watch was preseet to go off at the new boarding time. We now would have time to grab some diner!

List the correct spelling of the misspelled words below.

_____

_____

mom told me knot to delay going to the dentist she said I shoold try to pravent tooth dekay and fillings. Mom also tole me to brush and floss each nite before bed.

List the correct spelling of the misspelled words below.

_____

_____

138   Copyright © 2004 by High Noon Books. Permission granted to reproduce for classroom use.

Word Play

Name _____

Spelling Words

delete	defend	preset	defeat	deplete	delay
prerinse	decline	deform	preplan	decode	prevent
precede	prelaunch	preflight	bargain	again	certain

Crossword

Use the clues provided to fill in the crossword puzzle with your spelling words. Only use each word once.

Across
4. to change the shape or form
5. to change from code to plain text
8. to refuse
10. to get rid of
11. to rinse before
13. for sure
15. to empty out

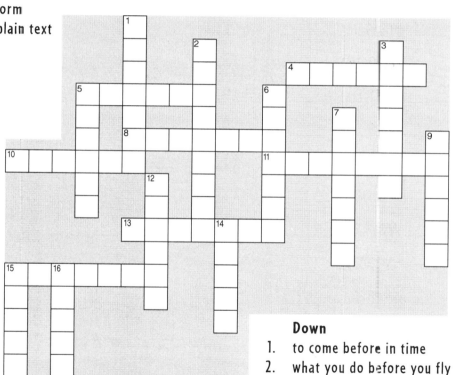

Down
1. to come before in time
2. what you do before you fly
3. to keep from happening
5. to win or beat
6. to plan before
7. a deal
9. to keep safe from harm
12. to set before
14. once more
15. to wait until a later time
16. what you do before you launch

Pretest

Name _____

Fold the first column under. Take the Pretest and write your answers in the second column. Unfold and self-check your answers. Study the words and write corrections in the third column.

Spelling Words	Take the Pretest	Write Corrections
1. chalk	1.	1.
2. walk	2.	2.
3. wallet	3.	3.
4. salt	4.	4.
5. wash	5.	5.
6. watch	6.	6.
7. talk	7.	7.
8. wander	8.	8.
9. swap	9.	9.
10. halt	10.	10.
11. fall	11.	11.
12. walnut	12.	12.
13. waltz	13.	13.
14. swamp	14.	14.
15. stalk	15.	15.
16. through	16.	16.
17. finally	17.	17.
18. favorite	18.	18.
Challenge Words		
19.	19.	19.
20.	20.	20.

➤ /ôl/ is often spelled *al* as in *fall*.
➤ /wô/ is often spelled *wa* as in *wasp*.

140

Copyright © 2004 by High Noon Books. Permission granted to reproduce for classroom use.

Word Sort

Name _____

Pattern Words Use the key words below to help you sort each pattern word by the indicated pattern.

Pattern Words
chalk   walk   wallet   salt   wash
watch   talk   wander   swap   halt
fall   walnut waltz   swamp   stalk

Words with *al* — tall

_____
_____
_____
_____

Words with *wa* — wasp

_____
_____
_____
_____

Read, Spell, Read!

High Frequency/Tricky Words Read each word out loud. Touch under each letter in each word, spell the word out loud, and read the word again. Then read the sentence. Underline the word in each sentence. Write the answer to the question using the underlined word.

through Pam told Gloria she would call when she was through with her chores. If it was not too late, they might still have time to make the show.
When will Pam call Gloria?

_____

finally Joe was happy he had finally learned how to play chess. He had been studying the rules for weeks, and the game now made sense.
What was Joe happy about?

_____

favorite Shana wore her favorite dress to the dance. All her friends would be there, and they hoped to have a great time!
What did Shana wear to the dance?

_____

141

LESSON 34 Reading, Writing & Spelling

Name _____

Spelling Words

chalk	walk	wallet	salt	wash
watch	talk	wander	swap	halt
fall	walnut	waltz	swamp	stalk

Dictionary & Vocabulary Connections

fall (fôl) *v.* **1.** To drop or come down: *She fell down.*
2. to be within a range: *The kids fall within three groups.*
3. To happen at a time: *My birthday will fall on Monday.*

1. Using the information above, what part or parts of speech is the word *fall?*

_____

2. Using all definitions above, create a web of synonyms for *fall.*
   You can use words or phrases.

   _____   (fall)   _____
   _____   _____

3. Which of the following could be the guide words for *fall?* _____
   a. fake   far   b. fade   fair   c. face   fad

4. Use definition #2 above and write your own sentence using the
   word *fall.* _____

   _____

5. Use definition #3 above and write your own sentence using the
   word *fall.* _____

   _____

6. List up to three words from the spelling list that come before and after
   fall in the dictionary.

   Before   After

   _____   _____

   _____   _____

   _____   _____

142   Copyright © 2004 by High Noon Books. Permission granted to reproduce for classroom use.

Name _____

Spelling Words

chalk	walk	wallet	salt	wash	watch
talk	wander	swap	halt	fall	walnut
waltz	swamp	stalk	through	finally	favorite

Word Paths

Connect one letter from each row to the next to find all the letters in one of your spelling words. Then write the word on the line provided. Each letter should be used once.

W	W	L	K
S	A	S	H
W	A	L	P
S	A	A	T

1. _____
2. _____
3. _____
4. _____

C	A	T	T	K
W	H	A	L	K
W	A	A	C	Z
S	T	L	L	H

5. _____
6. _____
7. _____
8. _____

W	W	N	K	E	
W	A	L	M	E	
S	A	L	D	P	T
T	A	A	L		R

9. _____
10. _____
11. _____
12. _____

W	H	L	N	L		
T	A	R	O		L	H
H	I	L	T	U	G	Y
F	A	N	A	U	T	

13. _____
14. _____
15. _____
16. _____

143

Pretest

Name _____

Fold the first column under. Take the Pretest and write your answers in the second column. Unfold and self-check your answers. Study the words and write corrections in the third column.

Spelling Words	Take the Pretest	Write Corrections
1. farmer	1.	1.
2. painter	2.	2.
3. helper	3.	3.
4. actor	4.	4.
5. planner	5.	5.
6. catcher	6.	6.
7. doctor	7.	7.
8. teacher	8.	8.
9. sailor	9.	9.
10. dancer	10.	10.
11. raptor	11.	11.
12. singer	12.	12.
13. driver	13.	13.
14. captor	14.	14.
15. traitor	15.	15.
16. together	16.	16.
17. surgeon	17.	17.
18. February	18.	18.

Challenge Words

19.	19.	19.
20.	20.	20.

➤ The suffix *-or* added to a root or base word means *one who*.
➤ The suffix *-er* added to a root or base word sometimes means *one who*.

Word Sort

Name _____

Pattern Words Use the key words below to help you sort each pattern word by the indicated pattern.

Pattern Words

farmer	painter	helper	actor	planner
catcher	doctor	teacher	sailor	dancer
raptor	singer	driver	captor	traitor

Words with -er — *waiter*

Words with -or — *traitor*

Read, Spell, Read!

High Frequency/Tricky Words Read each word out loud. Touch under each letter in each word, spell the word out loud, and read the word again. Then read the sentence. Underline the word in each sentence. Write the answer to the question using the underlined word.

together It was such a nice sunny day, Steve and Matt went to the zoo together. Dan stayed home because the painter was coming.
   What did Steve and Matt do?

_____

surgeon Jose's mom is a surgeon. She works close to home, but often his mom has to work nights because they need extra help.
   What job does Jose's mom have?

_____

February Pedro said he would teach Rafael to ski in February. He would be too busy before then to go to the slopes.
   When will Pedro have time to teach Rafael to ski?

_____

Reading, Writing & Spelling

Name _____

Spelling Words

farmer	painter	helper	actor	planner
catcher	doctor	teacher	sailor	dancer
raptor	singer	driver	captor	traitor

Writing — You are having a huge party, and you can invite ten friends. Who will you invite, and why? Use at least five of your spelling words in your writing below.

_____
_____
_____
_____
_____
_____
_____
_____
_____
_____

Check the following after you have proofread your writing.

☐ Check here if you proofread for **misspelled** words.
☐ Check here if you proofread for **words** you may have **left out** of your writing.
☐ Check here if you proofread for **punctuation**.
☐ Check here if you reread your writing to make sure it **makes sense**.

List below the spelling words from your list that you used in your writing.

_____
_____

List other words that were hard to spell. Proofread and check spellings.

_____
_____

Word Play

Name _____

Spelling Words

farmer	painter	helper	actor	planner	catcher
doctor	teacher	sailor	dancer	raptor	singer
driver	captor	traitor	together	surgeon	February

Word Find

Find the spelling words in the word find puzzle below. Circle each word.

A	L	H	D	R	I	V	E	R	A	I	S	E	T	S	C	T	T	E
R	E	R	T	F	E	E	O	E	N	T	D	O	R	T	P	M	T	R
A	O	E	R	A	A	T	I	C	L	T	R	S	I	T	P	R	P	P
H	T	T	H	C	C	R	R	T	I	S	U	R	G	E	O	N	O	O
L	R	N	M	O	A	R	M	E	R	R	N	H	E	L	P	E	R	R
P	T	I	D	T	C	H	O	E	H	E	R	R	D	T	A	P	I	F
C	F	A	E	L	E	T	L	T	R	C	T	T	O	B	L	E	C	E
D	R	P	R	R	O	A	O	P	C	N	T	R	E	A	P	R	E	T
R	C	I	P	G	A	C	C	G	E	A	C	A	N	A	R	O	C	U
F	E	B	R	U	A	R	Y	H	E	D	T	N	C	R	E	T	A	I
O	T	S	N	N	O	G	P	I	E	T	E	R	N	R	G	I	P	Y
G	Y	A	D	T	H	E	E	I	T	R	H	R	E	A	N	A	T	L
E	T	R	C	T	A	R	F	I	P	R	E	E	N	O	I	R	O	C
R	R	A	E	L	C	C	E	A	R	O	R	T	R	R	S	T	R	F
A	S	A	I	L	O	R	T	E	R	E	U	R	A	P	T	O	R	L
Y	O	D	C	A	E	E	O	R	E	T	U	A	D	A	R	G	R	R

Pretest
LESSONS 31-35 REVIEW

Name _____

Fold the first column under. Take the Pretest and write your answers in the second column. Unfold and self-check your answers. Study the words and write corrections in the third column.

Spelling Words	Take the Pretest	Write Corrections
1. improper	1.	1.
2. decrease	2.	2.
3. misprint	3.	3.
4. impose	4.	4.
5. misfile	5.	5.
6. impulse	6.	6.
7. prejudge	7.	7.
8. insane	8.	8.
9. preserve	9.	9.
10. injure	10.	10.
11. misplace	11.	11.
12. instinct	12.	12.
13. mistreat	13.	13.
14. defense	14.	14.
15. defy	15.	15.
16. because	16.	16.
17. through	17.	17.
18. together	18.	18.

Challenge Words

19.	19.	19.
20.	20.	20.

➤ The prefix *im–* or *in–* added to a root or base word means *not*.
➤ The prefix *mis–* added to a root or base word means *wrongly*.
➤ The prefix *de–* added to a root or base word means *opposite*.
➤ The prefix *pre–* added to a root or base word means *before*.

Name _____

Pattern Words Use the key words below to help you sort each pattern word by the indicated pattern.

Pattern Words				
improper	decrease	misprint	impose	misfile
impulse	prejudge	insane	preserve	injure
misplace	instinct	mistreat	defense	defy

Words with im- *immune*	Words with de- *decide*	Words with mis- *misshape*	Words with in- *inquire*	Words with pre- *preserve*

Read, Spell, Read!

High Frequency/Tricky Words Read each word out loud. Touch under each letter in each word, spell the word out loud, and read the word again. Then read the sentence. Underline the word in each sentence. Write the answer to the question using the underlined word.

because Rose did not want to learn to play the trumpet because she said it was too hard. She chose the flute instead.
Why did Rose not want to play the trumpet?
_____

through Jared ran through the mud as he rushed to class. The rain was pouring down, and now his socks would be wet all day.
Why were Jared's socks wet?
_____

together Katie and Matt like to draw together in class. They drew pictures for the teacher, and she put then up on the wall.
What do Katie and Matt like to do in class?
_____

149

LESSON 36

Reading, Writing & Spelling
LESSONS 31-35
REVIEW

Name _____

Spelling Words

improper	decrease	misprint	impose	misfile
improper	decrease	misprint	impose	misfile
impulse	prejudge	insane	preserve	injure
misplace	instinct	mistreat	defense	defy

Writing

You are asked to be teacher for the day. What might happen? Use at least five of your spelling words in your writing below.

_____

_____

_____

_____

_____

_____

_____

_____

_____

_____

Check the following after you have proofread your writing.

☐ Check here if you proofread for **misspelled** words.
☐ Check here if you proofread for **words** you may have **left out** of your writing.
☐ Check here if you proofread for **punctuation.**
☐ Check here if you reread your writing to make sure it **makes sense.**

List below the spelling words from your list that you used in your writing.

_____

_____

List other words that were hard to spell. Proofread and check spellings.

_____

_____

150   Copyright © 2004 by High Noon Books. Permission granted to reproduce for classroom use.

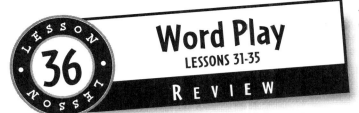

Word Play
LESSONS 31-35
REVIEW

Spelling Words

improper	decrease	misprint	impose	misfile	impulse
prejudge	insane	preserve	injure	misplace	instinct
mistreat	defense	defy	because	through	together

Crossword — Use the clues provided to fill in the crossword puzzle with your spelling words. Only use each word once.

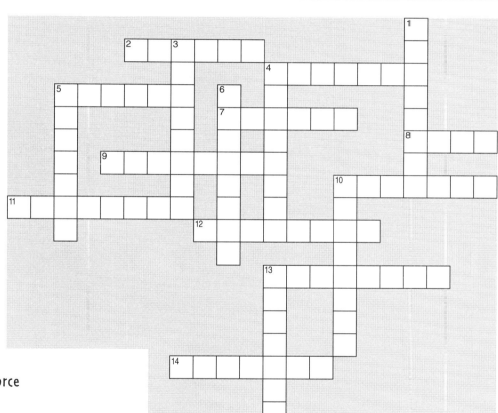

Across
2. to make by force
4. to file wrong
5. to get hurt
7. not sane
8. to go against
9. not suited to need
10. the act of keeping from getting hurt
11. to put in the wrong spot
12. a sudden wish
13. in a group
14. for the reason

Down
1. to judge before
3. to keep safe
4. to not treat right
5. to know to do something
6. to print wrong
10. to get less
13. in one side and out the other

151

Answer Key

Lesson 1 Page 9
Initial sh Words
shame, sheet, shock
Final sh Words
brush, crush, fresh
Initial th Words
thing, thud, thank
Final th Words
math, cloth
Initial wh Words
when, which, whisk, wheat

Page 11
1. shame
2. crush
3. fresh
4. wheat
5. shock
6. which
7. other
8. sheet
9. thud
10. whisk
11. thing
12. math
13. brush
14. when
15. cloth
16. thank

Lesson 2 Page 13
Initial ch Words
chain, champ, cheese
Final tch Words
scratch, twitch, switch, match, catch
Initial thr Words
three, throne, throw
Final ch Words
speech, beach
Initial ph Words
phone, phase

Page 14
1. cheese
2. twitch
3. match
4. three
5. often
6. switch
7. champ
8. enough
9. speech
10. scratch
11. phone
12. phase
13. catch
14. chain

1. throne
2. beach
3. throw

Page 15

Lesson 3 Page 17
Initial wr Words
wrong, wreath, wrist, write
Initial kn Words
knife, kneel, known, knock
Initial gn Words
gnaw, gnu, gnat
Final mb Words
limb, thumb, climb, lamb

Page 18
1. noun
2. large branch of a tree, jointed part of an animal, arm, leg, wing
3. b. like—line
6. **Before:** knock, known, gnaw, knife, gnu, climb, knee, gnat, lamb
   After: wrong, write, wreath, thumb, wrist

Page 19

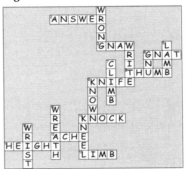

Lesson 4 Page 21
or Words
torch, north, porch, horse, thorn
sport, storm
ore Words
tore, score, shore, store, chore
oar Words
oar, soar, board

Page 22
I heard the hail **from** the **storm** pound down on the porch. Up the hill my **horse** heads for the **barn**. A loose **board** from my **gate** just flew into the wind. I **hope** the storm will move up the shore by the time night comes, or I will not be able **to** drive up **north** very soon.

The ending **score** from the game was proof **our** team had **really** lost. We did not **soar** to the top as some had thought we would. Football was over for the year, and even though we were a little sad, the **coach** said each of us should be a good **sport**. After the **torch** on the field was put out, we all went to **the** Sugar Shack store for a quick snack.

Lesson 4 Page 23
1. p ch or — porch
2. h s or e — shore
3. t ch or — torch
4. or st m — storm
5. or n th — thorn
6. ore st — store
7. e i t t l l — little
8. ore ch — chore
9. s oar — soar
10. oar d b — board
11. ore t — tore
12. or th n — north
13. ore sh — shore
14. ear h d — heard
15. or t s p — sport

Lesson 5 Page 25
er Words
merge, perch, fern, clerk, herd
ir Words
firm, skirt, first, swirl, girl
ur Words
blur, hurt, burn, curl, turn

Page 26
1. perch
2. burn
3. curl
4. fern
5. swirl
6. Turn
7. skirt
8. merge
9. hurt
10. blur
11. firm
12. girl
13. herd
14. clerk
15. first
16. fir, fit, sit, stir, it, is if, sir

Page 27
1. p **er** ch **perch**
2. g **ir** l
3. bl **ur** **blur**
4. f **er** n
5. m **er** ge **merge**
6. t **ur** n **turn**
7. sw **ir** l
8. sk **ir** t **skirt**
9. b **ur** n
10. h **er** d
11. h **ur** t **hurt**
12. f **ir** st
13. c **ur** l **curl**

1. wear
2. after
3. guard

Lesson 6 Page 29
au Words
haul, launch, vault
aw Words
drawn, lawn, hawk
oo Words
room, book, crook, pool, cook
oo Words
stood, spoon, smooth, swoop

Page 30
1. cook
2. stood
3. friend
4. launch
5. smooth
6. book
7. drawn
8. hour
9. swoop
10. gauge
11. room
12. vault
13. crook
14. haul

152

Answer Key

Lesson 6 Page 30
1. pool
2. spoon
3. lawn
3. hawk

Page 31

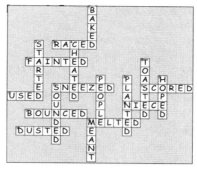

Lesson 7 Page 33
s Words
braces, causes, roses, bridges, horses, pieces, cases, places
es Words
pushes, teaches, dishes, itches, dresses, classes, lunches

Page 34
1. dishes
2. braces
3. pieces
4. lunches
5. pushes
6. cases
7. itches
8. roses
9. horses
10. classes
11. dresses
12. places
13. bridges
14. causes
15. teaches
16. tea, each, at, hat, sat, cheat, chat, set, cat, cats, ate, heat, eat, sheet, chest, ease, has, see, seat, sea, scat, ache aches

Page 35
1. braces
2. teaches
3. lunches
4. itches
5. classes
6. aisles
7. dresses
8. bridges
9. horses
10. places
11. heroes
12. causes
13. roses
14. pieces
15. oh
16. pushes

Lesson 8 Page 37
Words with ed
cheated, sounded, planted, fainted, dusted, toasted, started, melted
Words with drop e + ed
baked, used, sneezed, hoped, raced, scored, bounced

Lesson 9 Page 41
Words with drop e +ed
braked, joked, saved, judged, caged, faced, named
Words with doubling +ed
skipped, thinned, dipped, slammed, planned, nodded, trapped, dripped

Page 42
A slight noise **could** be heard in the **street** as Al **braked** to park the car by the house. Rose **skipped** to the door to see if her mom and dad were home. As she ran to see, the door **slammed** shut and locked her out! Now she was **trapped** in the yard!

Her ice cream **cone dripped** in the hot sun as Pam walked past the **caged** birds at the zoo. She walked and **joked** with her group. Far away Pam could see Ann with her group. Just as Pam **nodded** and **waved**, Ann turned and **faced** the bears. Pam would try to **meet** up with Ann at lunch to see if she was having fun.

Page 43
1. brake̸   ed   **braked**
2. dip **p** ed   **dipped**
3. slam **m** ed   **slammed**
4. **save̸** ed   saved
5. nod **d** ed   **nodded**
6. judge̸   ed   **judged**
7. skip **p** ed   **skipped**
8. **plan n** ed   planned
9. name̸   ed   **named**
10. **drip p** ed dripped
11. **trap p** ed trapped
12. thin **n** ed **thinned**
13. face̸   ed   **faced**

1. many
2. dealt
3. length

Lesson 10 Page 45
Words with ing
barking, brushing, rocking, cleaning, snowing, knowing, sleeping, playing, feeling, climbing
Words with drop e +ing
hiding, hiking, boring, baking, braking

Lesson 10 Page 46
1. verb
2. to have fun with, to have sport with, to act in jest, to act a role or part
3. a. plate—playa
6. **Before**: baking, barking, hiking, feeling, braking, brushing, cleaning, climbing, hiding, knowing, boring
After: snowing, sleeping, rocking

Page 47
1. s ing ow n   snowing
2. ie y d l   yield
3. ing b k a e̸   baking
4. ow kn ing   knowing
5. e̸ v y e   every
6. b ing or e̸   boring
7. cx o ing r   rocking
8. ing b k ar   barking
9. i e̸ h ing d   hiding
10. sh r ing u b   brushing
11. h ing k i e̸   hiking
12. l s p ee ing   sleeping
13. irg ea l n c   cleaning
14. c ing l ei   ceiling
15. nb l c ing i   climbing

Lesson 11 Page 49
Words with doubling + ing
shipping, planning, sitting, batting, spinning, winning, shopping, dripping
Words with drop e + ing
racing, voting, saving, making, writing, biking, diving

Page 50
1. diving
2. voting
3. shopping
4. writing
5. winning
6. batting
7. planning
8. saving
9. shipping
10. biking
11. sitting
12. spinning
13. racing
14. dripping
15. making
16. a, in, king, nag, man, gain, main, am, kin

Page 51
1. save̸
2. sit **t**
3. plan **n**   planning
4. shop **p**
5. vote̸   voting
6. bat **t**   batting
7. spin **n**   spinning
8. **drip p**
9. bike̸   biking
10. **dive̸**
11. **race̸**
12. write̸   writing
13. win **n**   winning

cont'd.

153

Answer Key

Lesson 11 Page 51 cont'd.
1. before
2. skiing
3. lying

Lesson 12 Page 53
s Words
laces, hoses, pages
es Words
scratches, branches, glasses
Doubling + Suffix
sipped, hitting, hugging, sledded, batted
Drop e + Suffix
phoning, taping, squeezed

Page 55
1. ur b ing n — burning
2. r b n es ch a — branches
3. l ss a es g — glasses
4. ea r m ing d — dreaming
5. t a b t ed — batted
6. p a_¢ ing t — taping
7. d s ed l ed — sledded
8. ing ph n o_¢ — phoning
9. p s p ed i — sipped
10. ee z squ ed — squeezed
11. le pp eo — people
12. n oi t p ed — pointed
13. f e b ore — before
14. t i h t ing — hitting
15. n y m a — many

Lesson 13 Page 57
Words with y
chilly, foamy, rainy, chunky, sticky, sleepy, lucky, dirty, cloudy
Words with doubling + y
muddy, sunny, foggy, blurry, funny, witty

Page 58
1. adjective
2. having the property of sticking, covered with an adhesive agent, warm, hard to do
3. c. stick—still
6. **Before:** dirty, chilly, chunky, sleepy, funny, foamy, cloudy, lucky, foggy, blurry
   After: sunny, witty

Page 59
1. witty
2. lucky
3. empty
4. foamy
5. funny
6. only
7. dirty
8. rainy
9. blurry
10. chilly
11. sleepy
12. sticky
13. chunky
14. muddy
15. foggy
16. cloudy

Lesson 14 Page 61
Words with ies
berries, copies, bunnies, hobbies, marries, kitties, pennies, worries, carries
Words with ies
carried, worried, jellied, hurried, married, copied

Page 62
1. kitties
2. hurried
3. worried
4. married
5. carries
6. pennies
7. bunnies
8. marries
9. hobbies
10. carried
11. worries
12. copies
13. copied
14. berries

1. married
2. jellied
3. carries
4. copied

Page 63
[word search puzzle]

Lesson 15 Page 65
Words with er
brighter, cleaner, deeper, thicker, hotter, dimmer
Words with est
weakest, greatest, smartest, brightest, meanest, greenest, maddest, wettest, biggest

Page 66
Sam wants to plant a **peach** tree next to the porch. **He bought** the **greenest** and **biggest** one he could find. The **first hole** he dug just wasn't deep **enough**, so he plans to dig a **deeper** hole this afternoon.

Yes, it will be a **better** night to spot the **many** stars in the sky. Last night we were only able to **see** the **brightest** star in the east, and it got **dimmer** as the night went on.

Page 67

Lesson 16 Page 69
Words with drop e + er
safer, ruder, nicer, cuter
Words with ier
dustier, happier, funnier
Words with drop e + est
nicest, cutest, safest, latest, palest
Words with iest
happiest, luckiest, funniest

Page 70
1. nicer
2. cutest
3. family
4. cuter
5. latest
6. safest
7. truly
8. funniest
9. palest
10. ruder
11. dustier
12. safer
13. happier
14. happiest

1. funnier
2. happier
3. mother
4. family

Page 71
1. t s ier d u — dustier
2. p h iest a p — happiest
3. n f n u iest — funniest
4. t u er c — cuter
5. f est a s — safest
6. n est i c — nicest
7. d r er u — ruder
8. n c i er — nicer
9. u iest l c k — luckiest
10. a f er s — safer
11. est l t a — latest
12. ier p a p h — happier
13. n f ier n u — funnier
14. a p est l — palest
15. u t est c — cutest

Lesson 17 Page 73
Words with Endings
melted, reaches, splashes, clapping, speeding
Compound Words
railroad, downstairs, toothbrush, airport, snowball, somewhere, necklace, highway, flashlight, cardboard

154

Answer Key

Page 75

Lesson 18 Page 77

Words + Suffix

fastest, greater, cleanest, blacker

Words with doubling + Suffix

madder, dimmest, wetter, bigger

Words with drop e + Suffix

tamest, later, closer, rudest

Words with y changed to i + Suffix

luckiest, dustiest, luckier

Page 78

1. dustiest
2. luckier
3. wetter
4. cleanest
5. greater
6. fastest
7. later
8. bigger
9. dimmest
10. tamest
11. blacker
12. luckiest
13. madder
14. rudest
15. closer
16. lose, loser, so, rose, close, role, ore, or, core

Lesson 18 Page 79

1. tame	est	**tamest**
2. mad	**d**	**madder**
3. **lucky**	**i**	luckier
4. **wet**	**t**	wetter
5. **fast**	est	fastest
6. black	er	**blacker**
7. **great**	er	greater
8. late	er	**later**
9. **big**	**g**	bigger
10. dusty	**i**	**dustiest**
11. clean	est	**cleanest**
12. dim	**m**	**dimmest**

1. better
2. mother
3. father

Lesson 19 Page 81

Words with un-

untie, unpack, unknown, unclean, unwrap, unlock, unlike

Words with dis-

discount, distrust, display, dislike, disturb, distrust, dissect, disrupt, dissolve

Page 82

Todd usually gets a **discount** at the **store** where his dad works. He was **very** happy when he saw a shirt on **display** that he liked. He had to wait for the clerk since he did not want to **disturb** her while she was waiting on someone else.

Rose had to **unlock** the front door **before** she could bring in her suitcase from the trunk of the car. She put her bag on the bed as she started to **unpack**. Rose tried not to **disturb** her pet rat who was sleeping by her bed.

Page 83

1. untie
2. unwrap
3. usage
4. unlock
5. display
6. usually
7. disturb
8. unclean
9. unpack
10. unlike
11. dissect
12. disrupt
13. unknown
14. distrust
15. dislike
16. discount

Lesson 20 Page 85

Words with un

unkind, unpaid, unreal, undress, unseen

Words with re

reprint, reheat, return, repair, remind, react, reread, repeat, respond, retreat

Page 86

1. verb, noun
2. send, put, carry back, a thing brought or sent back, a report on a vote
3. c. retro—revamp
6. **Before:** repair, reheat, react, retreat, remind, reread, repeat, respond
   After: unkind, unpaid, unreal, undress, unseen

Page 87

[word search puzzle]

Lesson 21 Page 89

Words with ly

mainly, lonely, nearly, friendly, slowly, proudly, bravely, smoothly

Words with ful

faithful, careful, handful, mouthful, awful, thankful, cheerful

Page 90

1. proudly
2. thankful
3. control
4. slowly
5. lonely
6. cheerful
7. awful
8. smoothly
9. nearly
10. careful
11. friendly
12. mainly
13. faithful
14. mouthful
15. bravely
16. brave, rave, are, rely, bar, bare, barely, ear, year, bear, able, real, ravel, lye, rye, by, be, lay, levy

Page 91

1. main	**ly**	**mainly**
2. **faith**	**ful**	faithful
3. friend	**ly**	**friendly**
4. **thank**	ful	thankful
5. **aw**	ful	awful
6. smooth	**ly**	**smoothly**
7. brave	**ly**	**bravely**
8. **proud**	**ly**	**proudly**
9. **near**	**ly**	nearly
10. hand	ful	**handful**
11. **care**	ful	careful
12. **cheer**	ful	cheerful
13. lone	**ly**	**lonely**

1. pretty
2. lose
3. cheerful

Lesson 22 Page 93

Words with less

careless, hopeless, speechless, harmless, painless, pointless, useless

Words with ness

freshness, sickness, kindness, witness, darkness, likeness, weakness, goodness

Page 94

1. speechless
2. painless
3. careless
4. witness
5. kindness
6. useless
7. pointless
8. sickness
9. weakness
10. hopeless
11. freshness
12. likeness
13. darkness
14. harmless
15. goodness

1. carry
2. column
3. weird

Page 95

1. are less c — careless
2. f sh ness r e — freshness
3. n less p ai — painless
4. ck ness s i — sickness
5. l i_e ness k — likeness
6. p s ch less ee — speechless
7. w ness k ea — weakness
8. oi p n t less — pointless
9. n d i ness k — kindness
10. s u_e less — useless
11. less o_e h p — hopeless

cont'd.

155

Answer Key

Lesson 22 Page 95 cont'd.
12. ness w t i   witness
13. h less m ar   harmless
14. ness ar k d   darkness
15. oo g ness d   goodness

Lesson 23 Page 97
VCCV Words
picnic, basket, object, pencil, blanket, fabric, insist
VCCV Words with double consonants
bottom, mitten, kitten, blossom, funnel, sudden, happen, pillow

Page 99

Lesson 24 Page 101
Words with un
unload, unkept, unwise, unfair, unlit
Words with dis
distract, disgust, distort, dismiss, disown
Words with re
refill, regroup, regard, redo, recall

Page 102
The unlit wick did not **distract** from the table setting, and a dim light from the hall cast a **glow** into the room. I **recall** how **pretty** Pam looked that night when she met Stan for **dinner**.

Mrs. Reed did not **dismiss** us on time for lunch again. Everyone felt it was **unfair**, but we also felt it **would** be **unwise** to state this to Mrs. Reed.

Page 103
1. disgust   9. unwise
2. distort   10. sure
3. regroup   11. redo
4. dismiss   12. unfair
5. unload   13. unkept
6. pretty   14. disown
7. unlit   15. always
8. recall   16. regard

Lesson 25 Page 105
VCCV Words
rabbit, insect, apron, napkin, public, problem

CV Words
chosen, crazy, human, music, depend, pilot, hotel, event, behind

Page 106
1. noun, adjective
2. one who flies a plane,
   a kind of light in a stove,
   a new TV show
3. a. pillow—pinch
6. **Before:** crazy, music, event, apron, napkin, chosen, human, depend, hotel, behind
   After: rabbit, problem, public

Page 107

[word search grid]

Lesson 26 Page 109
VC/V Words
finish, prison, planet, salad, cabin, punish, habit, shadow
V/CV Words
begin, event, silent, lady, depend, pupil, basic

Page 111

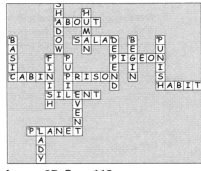

Lesson 27 Page 113
Open syllable + silent e syllable
became, decide, polite, behave, locate, female
Closed syllable + silent e syllable
reptile, costume, unsafe, advice, exhale, combine, athlete, suppose, volume

Page 114
The female **athlete** could not **compete** at the **meet**. It would have been **unsafe due** to her sprained wrist. They could not find **any** of the other girls to **replace** her.

Ross **tried** to **locate** the **costume** he wanted to **wear** for the party. It was **supposed** to be in the attic, but he couldn't find it. Tad gave him some good **advice** and told him to look again in the morning when it wouldn't be so dark.

Page 115

[word search grid]

Lesson 28 Page 117
VC/CV Words with r-controlled
enter, under, flutter, shelter, after, winter, sister
V/CV Words with r-controlled
over, vapor, voter, acorn, motor, driver
VC/V Words with r-controlled
river, lever

Page 118
1. noun
2. something that gives cover from the weather
   to protect or provide cover
3. b. sheer—shelve
6. **Before:** enter, over, flutter, after, acorn, lever, motor, driver, river
   After: under, vapor, winter, voter, sister

Page 119
1.	**shel**	**ter**	shelter
2.	o	**ver**	**over**
3.	**le**	ver	**lever**
4.	en	**ter**	**enter**
5.	**va**	por	**vapor**
6.	af	**ter**	**after**
7.	win	**ter**	**winter**
8.	mo	**tor**	**motor**
9.	sis	**ter**	**sister**
10.	**riv**	**er**	river
11.	un	**der**	**under**

1. recipe
2. today
3. quizzes

156

Answer Key

Lesson 29 Page 121
Words with re
recline, reface, restock, reflex, refresh
Words with dis
discuss, distaste
Words with un
untwist, unsent, unlock, uncap,
unused, unmet

Page 122

1. restock
2. replant
3. uncap
4. rerun
5. unused
6. reflex
7. distaste
8. unsent
9. unmet
10. recline
11. refresh
12. discuss
13. untwist
14. reface
15. untwist
16. is, wit, sun, sit, it,
stunt, win, in, tin,
sin, twist, nut, nuts,
twin

Page 123

1. p r e n t l a   replant
2. c r e l n i_e   recline
3. s dis a_e t t   distaste
4. s n u n t e   unsent
5. er n v e   never
6. ck l un o   unlock
7. t t c i dis n   distinct
8. f r e e r sh   refresh
9. re t s ck o   restock
10. un ed u_e s   unused
11. un t t i s w   untwist
12. re x e f l   reflex
13. ss dis u c   discuss
14. c e n s l i e   license
15. e t un m   unmet

Lesson 30 Page 125
VC/CV Words
plenty, puppet, budget, wisdom,
adjust, helmet, cactus
V/CV Words
item, protect, wages, sofa
VC/V Words
credit, second, basic, solid

Page 126

1. puppet
2. plenty
3. budget
4. basic
5. item
6. sofa
7. adjust
8. wisdom
9. credit
10. wages
11. helmet
12. cactus
13. solid
14. protect
15. second

1. sofa
2. cactus
3. puppet

Page 127

1. wisdom
2. solid
3. wages
4. sofa
5. adjust
6. today
7. item
8. plenty
9. protect
10. puppet
11. cactus
12. credit
13. budget
14. never
15. any
16. helmet

Lesson 31 Page 129
Words with im
impress, impede, impulse, impale,
improve, import, imprint
Words with in
involve, infect, intense, inept, insult,
inspect, infest

Page 130

1. immune
2. inspect
3. improve
4. interest
5. infest
6. inept
7. import
8. impulse
9. intense
10. involve
11. impale
12. insult
13. aspirin
14. around
15. imprint
16. print, tin, in, mint,
pint, rim, trim, trip
tip, rip, mit, nip,
pin, prim

Page 131

1. **in** **volve** involve
2. **im** **pulse** impulse
3. im print **imprint**
4. **im** **pede** impede
5. **in** **sult** insult
6. **in** **ept** inept
7. in spect **inspect**
8. **im** **prove** improve
9. **im** **press** impress
10. **in** **fest** infest
11. im port **import**
12. **in** **tense** intense

1. import
2. immune
3. interest

Lesson 32 Page 133
Words with mis
misuse, misspell, mistake, misprint,
misdial, mistrust, mislead, misjudge,
mismatch
Words with pre
prepaid, prebake, pretend, preheat,
prefer, precut

Page 134

1. pretend
2. prefer
3. mistake
4. prebake
5. prepaid
6. misjudge
7. precut
8. mislead
9. misspell
10. misdial
11. symbol
12. mismatch
13. misuse
14. misprint
15. mistrust

1. prebake
2. mistrust
3. symbol

Page 135

1. k b a_e pre   prebake
2. h pre t ea   preheat
3. u_e mis s   misuse
4. k t a_e mis   mistake
5. ough o th r   thorough
6. u dge mis j   misjudge
7. mis r s t t u   mistrust
8. e t n pre d   pretend
9. a d l mis i   misdial
10. l d mis ea   mislead
11. f pre er   prefer
12. au b e e c s   because
13. mis s ll p e   misspell
14. mis tch a m   mismatch
15. ai p d pre   prepaid

Lesson 33 Page 137
Words with de
delete, delay, decode, defend,
decline, defeat, deform, deplete
Words with pre
prerinse, prevent, preset, precede,
prelaunch, preplan, preflight

Page 138

As we boarded the plane the **pilot**
gave us some **preflight** news. **There**
would be a short ten-minute **delay**
while they cleared the runway. The
alarm on my watch was **preset** to go
off at the new boarding time. We
now would have time to grab some
dinner!

Mom told me **not** to delay going to
the dentist. She said I **should** try to
prevent tooth **decay** and fillings.
Mom also told me to brush and floss
each **night** before bed.

157

Answer Key

Page 139

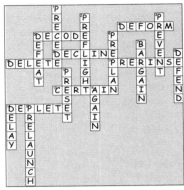

Lesson 34 Page 141

Words with al
chalk, fall, talk, salt, halt, stalk, walnut, wallet, waltz
Words with wa
watch, walk, wash, wander, swamp

Page 142

1. verb
2. drop, come down,
   to be within a range,
   to happen at a time
3. a. fake—far
6. **Before:** chalk
   After: walk, wallet, salt, wash, watch, talk, wander, swap, halt, walnut, waltz, swamp, stalk

143

1. walk
2. salt
3. wash
4. swap
5. chalk
6. watch
7. waltz
8. stalk
9. wander
10. wallet
11. swamp
12. talk
13. walnut
14. through
15. halt
16. finally

Lesson 35 Page 145

Words with er
farmer, catcher, painter, singer, helper, teacher, driver, planner, dancer
Words with or
raptor, doctor, actor, sailor, captor, traitor

Page 147

[word search grid]

Lesson 36 Page 149

Words with im
improper, impulse, impose
Words with de
decrease, defense, defy
Words with mis
misplace, misprint, mistreat, misfile
Words with in
instinct, insane, injure
Words with pre
prejudge, preserve

Page 151

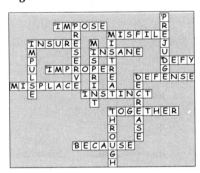

158

Posttest

Name _____

Date _____

Score _____

1. _____	11. _____
2. _____	12. _____
3. _____	13. _____
4. _____	14. _____
5. _____	15. _____
6. _____	16. _____
7. _____	17. _____
8. _____	18. _____
9. _____	19. _____
10. _____	20. _____

Spelling Patterns or Words That Need More Practice

APPENDIX B

Stimulus Sentences

1. Before you start, prompt students to think about the sound-spelling relationships they have learned.
2. Say the word.
3. Use the word in a sentence.
4. Repeat the word.
5. Ask students to say the word to themselves and write the word.
6. Students should self-check the pretest. It is recommended that students review their errors on the posttest.

Lesson 1–REVIEW

1. shame — It is a shame that Ann is sick.
2. whisk — I used a whisk to beat the eggs.
3. thud — The heavy box dropped with a thud.
4. brush — Don't forget to brush your teeth every night.
5. crush — They first crush the grapes in order to made wine.
6. when — When can we go to the movies?
7. wheat — Wheat flour is used to make bread.
8. math — We learned to add fractions in math today.
9. thank — She remembered to thank everyone who came to her party.
10. cloth — I'm going to the fabric store to get cloth for the drapes.
11. which — Which swimsuit do you want to buy?
12. thing — I can't fit one more thing into this suitcase.
13. sheet — The letter she sent fit on one sheet of paper.
14. shock — It was a shock to find out that George was moving.
15. fresh — We have fresh or frozen strawberries.
16. other — You can ride with Pam, and I will ride in the other car.
17. breath — Amy was short of breath after she ran a mile.
18. breathe — I could hear the baby breathe in the crib.

Lesson 2–REVIEW

1. chain — Rose lost her charm when the necklace chain broke.
2. scratch — The toy car made a scratch on the table.
3. phone — Becky wants a phone for her room.
4. three — Jennifer has three children.
5. speech — Matt made a speech to the class.
6. throne — The king sat on his throne.
7. champ — The champ waved to the crowd.
8. twitch — I could see the rabbit's ear twitch.
9. graph — The assignment is to make a graph.
10. switch — Steve and I want to switch bedrooms.
11. beach — We played in the waves at the beach.
12. match — The tennis match lasted three hours.
13. cheese — Angie wants cheese on her sandwich.
14. throw — The throw to second base was just a little too late
15. catch — We played catch in the park.
16. often — How often do you have homework?
17. enough — There are enough cookies for everyone.
18. phase — The next phase of the project is to create the presentation.

Lesson 3–REVIEW

1. wrong — Robert spelled one word wrong on his test.
2. knock — Remember to knock before going into her room.
3. limb — The limb on the tree broke during the windstorm.
4. gnu — Jesse took a picture of a gnu grazing in the field at the zoo.
5. thumb — During art today we got to turn thumbprints into animals.
6. knife — Remember to put a fork, spoon, and knife by each place setting.
7. wreath — The wreath hung on the front door.
8. wrist — Steve broke his wrist playing ball.
9. kneel — Ryan was asked to kneel as he received his award.

10. gnat — The gnat was so small you could hardly see it.
11. known — How much is known about the new student?
12. gnaw — The dog likes to gnaw on a bone.
13. climb — Michaela asked if she could climb the big tree.
14. write — Our group has to write an essay about the Civil War.
15. lamb — Ross planned to buy the baby lamb for his farm.
16. answer — Please answer the phone if it rings.
17. height — Erik's height is 6'3".
18. ache — Mom had an ache in her back after planting all day.

Lesson 4—REVIEW

1. torch — Pedro lit each torch along the path.
2. store — I'll go to the store to get some milk.
3. oar — Rosa lost an oar while rowing.
4. chore — Megan's least favorite chore was to clean the toilet.
5. porch — The porch light was out, so it was hard to see the door.
6. sport — Baseball is my favorite sport.
7. soar — I can see the Bald Eagle soar over the mountains.
8. score — What was the score at half time?
9. horse — Maggie boards her horse in the country.
10. shore — Driftwood washed up onto the shore.
11. storm — The storm brought with it lots of thunder and rain.
12. board — It is time to board the plane.
13. tore — Ryan tore his shirt climbing over the fence.
14. north — I live north of the school.
15. thorn — The rose's thorn stuck me.
16. little — The bike was too little for me to ride.
17. heard — I heard that you plan to audition for the show.
18. sugar — I would like cream and sugar in my coffee, please.

Lesson 5—REVIEW

1. merge — You need to merge to the center lane.
2. perch — The robin found a thin branch to perch on in the elm tree.
3. firm — How firm are the oranges?
4. skirt — Katie's skirt was covered in bows!
5. blur — All I could see was a blur through the foggy windshield.
6. hurt — Did you hurt yourself when you fell off your bike?
7. first — Steven was the first to cross the finish line.
8. fern — A fern hangs in the family room.
9. swirl — When I paint I swirl the colors together on the canvas.
10. burn — Be careful not to burn yourself on the hot stove.
11. curl — Mom will curl my hair before the talent show.
12. girl — A new girl moved across the street.
13. turn — When will it be my turn to play the video game?
14. clerk — The clerk at the store helped me find the eggs.
15. herd — A herd of cattle ran to the corral.
16. after — Can you come over after school?
17. wear — What will you wear to the party?
18. guard — The guard at the bank had to stand most of the day.

Lesson 6—REVIEW

1. haul — I plan to haul the garbage to the dump on Saturday.
2. spoon — I need a spoon for my ice cream.
3. lawn — Matt needs to mow the lawn this afternoon.
4. smooth — The edge of the nickel felt smooth.
5. launch — They plan to launch the shuttle soon.
6. stood — Mark stood by the door.
7. pool — Ashley has a pool in her backyard.
8. cook — I plan to cook spaghetti for dinner.
9. hawk — I saw a hawk fly over the field.
10. swoop — Alison saw a vulture swoop and catch a mouse.
11. crook — The crook stole rugs from the store.
12. room — How large is your bedroom?
13. vault — The bank kept all their money in a vault.
14. book — I can't wait to start reading my new book.
15. drawn — Many trees were drawn on the mural.
16. friend — My best friend is Rachel.
17. hour — The hour hand on the clock is pointing to three.
18. gauge — Dad used the tire gauge to see if the tires needed air.

Lesson 7

1. braces   I will need to get braces to straighten my teeth.
2. itches   My arm itches from the bee sting.
3. roses   My roses are in full bloom.
4. horses   How many horses are in the barn?
5. classes   Two new classes will be added at our school.
6. cases   I bought two cases of soda at the store.
7. pushes   Ms. Ercolini gave everyone ten pushes on the swing.
8. teaches   Mrs. Maher teaches reading to different groups all day.
9. dishes   I have not washed the dirty dishes.
10. places   There are lots of new places we can go on vacation.
11. dresses   Elizabeth bought two dresses on sale today.
12. causes   There are many causes as to why no one showed up.
13. lunches   I made all the lunches last night.
14. bridges   Shawn ended up crossing two bridges on his way home.
15. pieces   Are there many pieces in the puzzle?
16. oh   Oh, I can see her now!
17. aisles   There are many aisles in the new store.
18. heroes   The soldiers were honored as heroes.

Lesson 8

1. cheated   Two students cheated on the test.
2. hoped   She hoped to win the contest.
3. fainted   Mrs. Sullivan fainted in the heat.
4. planted   Mr. Phillips has planted corn every year.
5. raced   I raced my brother to the front door.
6. used   I used towels to clean up the mess.
7. toasted   Marie toasted a bagel for breakfast.
8. baked   Gina baked cookies after school.
9. melted   The candy melted in my mouth.
10. sounded   The drums sounded loud from upstairs.
11. sneezed   I sneezed three times after smelling the flowers in the garden.
12. dusted   Mom dusted the bookshelves.
13. bounced   Matt bounced the ball outside.
14. started   Dan started the car to warm it up.
15. scored   Randy scored eight points in the basketball game.
16. people   There are three people going camping with us.

17. meant   Tyler meant to knock before opening the door.
18. niece   My niece will baby-sit for us tonight.

Lesson 9

1. braked   Zack braked to avoid hitting the deer.
2. dipped   Luke dipped his French fry in ketchup.
3. planned   My family planned a long vacation.
4. trapped   Jake was trapped outside because he forgot his key.
5. saved   The sales saved me lots of money.
6. skipped   I skipped breakfast because I was late for school.
7. thinned   James thinned the vines in the the pumpkin patch.
8. caged   The caged parakeet chirped all day.
9. slammed   Sam slammed the door shut.
10. nodded   Sara nodded at me from across the room.
11. faced   Robert faced many challenges by being in a wheel chair.
12. named   Terrill was named after his father.
13. joked   Dad joked with me about going to the playground.
14. judged   They judged the contestants on their talent.
15. dripped   The candle dripped onto the table.
16. many   How many of you went to the movies?
17. length   I shortened the length of my dress.
18. dealt   Each player was dealt five cards.

Lesson 10

1. barking   The barking dog woke us up.
2. rocking   The new mother enjoyed the rocking chair.
3. hiding   A little kitten was hiding under the bush.
4. hiking   Hiking at the beach is fun.
5. knowing   Knowing the rules is an important part of learning a sport.
6. playing   The kids are playing ball outside.
7. boring   The movie was really boring.
8. snowing   It is so cold that it is snowing.
9. baking   My mom is baking a cake for dessert.
10. braking   You could hear the squeal of the tires braking.
11. brushing   Brushing your teeth twice a day is important.
12. cleaning   The shed needs lots of cleaning.
13. sleeping   Renee is sleeping soundly in the crib.

14. feeling — Are you feeling better?
15. climbing — Ross really enjoys climbing trees.
16. every — Every child should learn to read.
17. yield — I had to yield to the driver who was crossing in front of me.
18. ceiling — The tree was too high for the ceiling.

Lesson 11

1. making — What are you making in your art class?
2. biking — I was biking down the path.
3. shipping — The store promised to not charge me for shipping.
4. sitting — Four children are sitting on the bench.
5. spinning — The merry-go-round kept spinning.
6. racing — Racing cars is a dangerous sport.
7. voting — Tomorrow we will be voting for a candidate.
8. shopping — Let's go shopping for new jackets.
9. saving — I hope you are saving some money.
10. writing — Sally is writing a children's book.
11. diving — I saw my teacher driving to school.
12. dripping — Ice cream was dripping on the floor.
13. planning — We are planning a picnic for next Saturday.
14. batting — Batting practice went well today on the field.
15. winning — Winning is not as important as having fun playing.
16. before — Do not eat your dessert before lunch.
17. skiing — David is skiing down the mountain.
18. lying — I hope you are telling the truth and not lying to me.

Lesson 12–REVIEW LESSON

1. branches — Three branches broke during the storm last night.
2. heated — They heated the hot tub to a comfortable temperature.
3. hugging — Grandma would not stop hugging me!
4. phoning — She said she will be phoning the team tonight.
5. taping — Be very careful taping up the package.
6. sledded — I sledded down the hill on a sled.
7. burning — The wood was burning too quickly to keep the fire going.
8. batted — I batted three times in this game.
9. glasses — My glasses broke, and now I have a hard time reading.

10. squeeze — Be careful not to squeeze the ketchup bottle too hard!
11. dreaming — I was dreaming of my wedding.
12. laces — Your laces are untied.
13. pointed — The teacher pointed to the country on the map.
14. sipped — Dad slowly sipped his coffee
15. hitting — The ball keeps hitting the fence.
16. people — There are only 500 people in our town.
17. many — How many of you are going bowling?
18. before — Study before you take the test!

Lesson 13

1. chilly — It was a chilly February morning.
2. funny — The cartoons were very funny.
3. muddy — The lot was muddy after the storm.
4. rainy — Tomorrow will be another rainy day.
5. chunky — I don't like chunky peanut butter.
6. sunny — I want to go live in a sunny place.
7. foggy — San Francisco can be very foggy in the mornings.
8. sleepy — Are you sleepy today after going to bed late?
9. dirty — I will need to wash the dirty clothes.
10. foamy — The foamy soap got things clean.
11. cloudy — It was a cloudy dark day on Monday.
12. sticky — I need to wash my sticky fingers.
13. lucky — Which lucky kid will be chosen?
14. blurry — My vision is blurry without my glasses.
15. witty — He is a charming, witty old man.
16. only — There is only one cookie left.
17. library — The library is full of books.
18. empty — My glass is empty.

Lesson 14

1. berries — There are lots of berries on the vine.
2. married — I plan to get married in July.
3. bunnies — The bunnies hopped on the lawn.
4. marries — If Andre marries Kim, we will be related.
5. carried — I carried the heavy box up the stairs.
6. pennies — I only have two pennies in my purse.
7. carries — I hope she carries the groceries for me.
8. worried — I am worried that we might be late to the meeting.
9. jellied — The jellied ham looked delicious.
10. hurried — Kristina hurried home after school.
11. copies — How many copies of that article do you need?

12. hobbies — One of Stephanie's hobbies is sewing.
13. copied — I copied that poem for you.
14. kitties — There are three kitties for sale.
15. worries — I don't have any worries about safety.
16. above — The skyscraper towers above us.
17. chief — The Chief of Police has a hard job.
18. ninth — There were three runs in the ninth inning of the game.

Lesson 15

1. brighter — There is one star that looks brighter than the rest.
2. greatest — That was the greatest thing you ever did for me!
3. hotter — It is hotter in the cities south of us.
4. maddest — Maggie was the maddest student in the group.
5. brightest — There is the brightest star in the sky.
6. biggest — Don't take the biggest piece of cake.
7. weakest — She was the weakest tennis player.
8. smartest — You are the smartest kid in the class.
9. deeper — You need to dig that hole deeper.
10. wettest — The rain has made this the wettest year ever.
11. thicker — I need a thicker lining in my coat.
12. meanest — He is the meanest kid at school.
13. dimmer — The dimmer switch allows me to vary how much light is given off.
14. greenest — That is the greenest lawn I have ever seen!
15. cleaner — Your room needs to be cleaner before you can go outside!
16. better — You did a better job on your essay this time.
17. seize — He had to seize his sword to fight the battle.
18. siege — The siege of the throne was important news!

Lesson 16

1. dustier — The piano was dustier than the shelves.
2. safer — The ride with the seatbelts looks much safer.
3. happiest — This is the happiest I have ever been.
4. luckiest — Sonlay is the luckiest kid in the world!
5. safest — Jean drove the safest route.
6. ruder — That man was even ruder than I remember.
7. happier — I am much happier that you will stay in California.

8. palest — When Michaela had the flu, she was the palest I have ever seen her.
9. latest — Let's catch the latest bus home.
10. funniest — That is the funniest movie I have ever seen!
11. nicer — That teacher was much nicer than the one we had last week.
12. funnier — Your joke was funnier than the one that Lou shared.
13. cuter — That puppy is much cuter now that it has had a bath.
14. nicest — Mrs. Tubach is one of the nicest teachers at school.
15. cutest — Megan just got the cutest haircut!
16. mother — My mother works three days a week at the dry cleaners.
17. truly — I am truly thankful for my friends.
18. family — There are five people in my family.

Lesson 17

1. railroad — The railroad tracks are right behind my house.
2. yourself — Help yourself to more rice.
3. airport — I will drive to the airport and leave my car there.
4. bathroom — Wash your hands in the bathroom.
5. snowball — We had a snowball fight in the front yard.
6. toothbrush — I brought my toothbrush on our trip.
7. downstairs — The laundry room is downstairs.
8. highway — Highway 12 will lead you to Denver.
9. playground — There are swings on our playground.
10. somewhere — I lost my earring somewhere on the airplane.
11. earthquake — Did you feel the earthquake?
12. flashlight — I used my flashlight to find the campsite in the dark.
13. cardboard — Get more cardboard boxes for packing.
14. necklace — I got a pearl necklace as a gift.
15. snowflake — The snowflake melted on my tongue.
16. father — My father works at the grocery store.
17. quiet — You need to be quiet in the library.
18. quite — It is quite a long walk to my house.

Lesson 18–REVIEW LESSON

1. blacker — The night sky in the forest looked blacker.
2. fastest — I found the fastest route home.
3. luckier — Tara is luckier than Adam.
4. bigger — My room is much bigger than yours.

5. rudest — She is the rudest person I have met.
6. hottest — June 10th was the hottest day of the year.
7. tamest — Leo is the tamest of the lions at the zoo.
8. madder — She became madder at the waitress as the night went on.
9. dimmest — That light is on the dimmest setting.
10. dustiest — The family room is the dustiest room in the house.
11. reddest — Sara has the reddest checks in the group.
12. wetter — If you get wetter, you'll feel cooler.
13. later — I'll stop by later this afternoon.
14. greater — There is a greater need warm clothes.
15. cleanest — Samuel has the cleanest room in the house.
16. better — You will do better next time.
17. mother — My mother takes me to school.
18. father — My father works at his computer most of the day.

Lesson 19

1. untie — Katie asked me to untie her shoelaces.
2. dislike — I dislike mushrooms on my pizza.
3. disturb — The sign said, "Do not disturb."
4. unclean — The hotel room was very unclean.
5. unlike — Unlike yesterday, today we will be able to practice outside.
6. discount — The cashier gave me a discount because I bought so many liters.
7. unpack — I will unpack my suitcase tomorrow.
8. distrust — I distrust the city government.
9. unwrap — Dan wanted to unwrap the present before everyone was there.
10. disrupt — The bell will disrupt the class.
11. display — There were lots of flowers on display at the department store.
12. unknown — The meaning of that word was unknown to all of us.
13. dissect — We were asked to dissect the seed in biology class.
14. unlock — Don't forget to unlock the sliding glass door before you leave.
15. dissolve — I watched the sugar dissolve in the glass of water.
16. very — I am very happy that today is Friday.
17. usage — The irresponsible usage of the computer caused it to breakdown.
18. usually — I usually take the bus to school.

Lesson 20

1. unkind — Someone at recess was unkind to me.
2. reheat — I will reheat the pizza for dinner.
3. remind — Please remind me to call her after church.
4. repeat — The doctor said to repeat the exercises daily.
5. respond — I wanted to respond when the question was asked
6. reprint — They will reprint the poem in the newspaper.
7. return — Please return the jacket you borrowed from me.
8. react — Miguel did not react when the older boy teased him.
9. unreal — The flower was so perfect, it looked unreal.
10. unseen — We bought the car sight unseen.
11. unpaid — The library sent me a bill for the unpaid late fee.
12. repair — The handle on my suitcase needs repair.
13. reread — That book was so good, I want to reread it at a later date.
14. undress — I went to my room to undress for bed.
15. retreat — We are going on a family retreat with our church.
16. sure — I sure like the taste of that new soda!
17. guess — My guess was too low, and I didn't win the prize.
18. hoarse — My teacher's voice got hoarse.

Lesson 21

1. mainly — We are mainly going to visit museums on this trip.
2. faithful — Beth is a faithful friend.
3. proudly — I proudly fly an American flag outside my house.
4. bravely — The fireman bravely ran into the burning house.
5. awful — That medicine had an awful taste.
6. friendly — My new neighbor is friendly.
7. careful — Be careful to watch for snakes.
8. mouthful — Don't talk with a mouthful of food!
9. lonely — I was lonely on my business trip.
10. thankful — I am thankful for my family.
11. nearly — I nearly hit the bus as it swerved.
12. slowly — I slowly crossed the street watching for cars.
13. handful — Derek grabbed a handful of peanuts.
14. smoothly — Everything went smoothly as planned.

15. cheerful   Margo is cheerful about her new job.
16. pretty   She looks pretty in pink.
17. lose   I don't want to lose my watch.
18. control   We will control the boat's speed.

Lesson 22

1. careless   I made a careless mistake on my math test.
2. sickness   Danny's sickness kept him out of school for a couple of months.
3. speechless   I was speechless when they called my name for the award.
4. pointless   It is pointless to argue with the policeman.
5. weakness   A weakness in my knee is making it hard to climb stairs.
6. freshness   You could taste the freshness of bread that was served with dinner.
7. kindness   Kelly's kindness was very much appreciated.
8. harmless   That snake is harmless.
9. darkness   I need to be home before darkness falls.
10. useless   The tool you brought me is useless for cutting iron.
11. hopeless   Brian felt like finding another job was hopeless.
12. witness   Jane was a witness to the crime.
13. painless   Claire said the shot was painless.
14. likeness   She bore a shocking likeness to her cousin.
15. goodness   Grandma shouted, "My goodness, you have grown!"
16. carry   Will you help me carry the groceries?
17. weird   I saw someone with a weird hairdo.
18. column   Add up all the figures in this column.

Lesson 23

1. bottom   I found the book at the bottom of the box.
2. kitten   The mother cat cleaned her kitten.
3. pencil   Rita uses a pencil to write the list.
4. funnel   Use a funnel to pour juice in the can.
5. happen   We watched the circus happen before our eyes.
6. mitten   Look for the mitten on the shelf.
7. basket   Jack put fresh peaches in the basket.
8. blossom   The blossoms bloomed on the trees.
9. sudden   The earthquake was sudden.
10. pillow   I sleep well on my new pillow.
11. picnic   The class picnic was held outside.

12. object   There are many pretty objects in that store.
13. blanket   The blanket kept Simon warm at night.
14. fabric   I made a coat with red fabric.
15. insist   Mom said, "I insist that you come in for lunch."
16. always   Lynn always does her homework right after school.
17. angle   The math teacher drew a right angle on the board.
18. angel   Raj said, "You are an angel to help me cook!"

Lesson 24–REVIEW LESSON

1. unload   Steven helped me unload the car.
2. distract   Do not distract your sister from finishing her homework.
3. unkept   Joe was disappointed with his friend because of the unkept promise.
4. redo   Redo your homework to get full credit.
5. disown   I wanted to disown my friend after she embarrassed me.
6. refill   Johnell went refill his popcorn bag.
7. disgust   Mrs. Capps looked with disgust at the mess.
8. distort   That mirror tends to distort your image.
9. unwise   It is unwise to walk on that street at night.
10. recall   The car manufacturer plans to recall that model next week.
11. regroup   The students will need to regroup.
12. regard   Mr. Wright saved the drowning boy without regard to his own safety.
13. dismiss   The teachers will dismiss the class early today because of the field trip.
14. unlit   There was only one unlit candle on the table.
15. unfair   The crowd thought the referee made an unfair decision.
16. sure   I am sure I will like this job.
17. pretty   The girls all looked pretty dressed in their party clothes.
18. always   Always remember to knock before you come in.

Lesson 25

1. rabbit   The rabbit was part of the magician's act.

167

2. crazy   It would be crazy to try to get into the show this late.

3. music   Mr. Mahoney played classical music while we worked.

4. pilot   The pilot landed the plane smoothly.

5. event   There is already an event scheduled for the park that afternoon.

6. insect   I saw an insect crawl along that log.

7. apron   You are required to wear an apron when working at the counter.

8. napkin   Did you put a napkin by each place?

9. public   The public library is only open one night a week.

10. problem   She had a problem at school today.

11. chosen   I was not chosen for the baseball team.

12. human   We are studying about the human body.

13. depend   You can depend on Katie to give you a ride home each day.

14. hotel   My aunt is staying at the hotel down the street.

15. behind   The house behind mine is being painted yellow.

16. upon   Once upon a time there lived a beautiful fairy in an enchanted castle.

17. reign   The king's reign lasted twenty years.

18. genius   Gabriel is considered a genius.

Lesson 26

1. finish   I want to finish the last chapter before I go to bed.

2. planet   We live on planet Earth.

3. shadow   The oak tree cast a beautiful shadow onto the pavement in the park.

4. lady   The lady next door baby-sits for me.

5. punish   My mom said she would have to punish me if I did not clean my room today.

6. habit   Melissa has a habit of chewing gum all the time.

7. begin   I will begin the essay after dinner.

8. silent   The house became silent after all the children had gone to sleep.

9. cabin   I bought a cabin up at the lake.

10. basic   Abby needs to take the basic math class before she enrolls in Algebra.

11. prison   Jake was sent to prison after he was caught robbing a store.

12. event   The event will start at 3:00 PM.

13. salad   I made a large salad for dinner.

14. depend   You can depend on Joan.

15. pupil   I wanted to help the pupil who was having a hard time with her math.

16. about   It took about five hours to get home.

17. human   There are many human beings on the earth.

18. pigeon   Cheryl could see a pigeon on the windowsill across the street.

Lesson 27

1. became   George became the star on the football team.

2. decide   It was hard for Steven to decide what college to go to.

3. polite   Rob is always polite when he eats at our house.

4. reptile   Snakes are part of the reptile family.

5. costume   What costume are you wearing for Halloween?

6. behave   Did the children behave well?

7. unsafe   It is unsafe to leave medicine where young children can find it.

8. exhale   Exhale slowly when you are singing.

9. combine   They want to combine our classes this afternoon for the assembly.

10. athlete   Who got the Athlete of the Year award?

11. female   Samantha is the best female runner on the track team.

12. advice   I asked my mom for her advice as to what I should wear tonight.

13. volume   If you become a movie star, you will receive a large volume of fan mail.

14. locate   I am trying to locate my sister.

15. suppose   I don't suppose you remembered to bring the hair dryer?

16. any   I don't have any shorts with me.

17. rhythm   That song had a great rhythm.

18. rhyme   Erik read the rhyme for the class.

Lesson 28

1. enter   I saw her enter from the back door.

2. over   Sam kicked the ball over the fence.

3. under   The napkin fell under the table.

4. flutter   I watched the butterfly flutter away.

5. river   It was fun to canoe down the river.

6. shelter   The canopy provided shelter from the rain.

7. vapor   Water vapor rose from the tea kettle.

8. after   After school you need to go right home.

9. winter   Winter is the coldest time of year.

10. voter   Only one voter showed up at the poles.
11. lever   The flight attendant pulled the lever to lock the door.
12. acorn   I found an acorn under the oak tree.
13. sister   My sister is three years old.
14. motor   The motor on the lawn mower broke.
15. driver   The driver parked too close to the truck.
16. today   Today is Friday.
17. quizzes   We have three math quizzes each month.
18. recipe   I want the recipe for the cake she made.

Lesson 29

1. recline   Dad likes to recline in his chair.
2. unbend   It was hard to unbend the handlebars.
3. restock   We were told to restock the canned goods first.
4. replant   I will replant more tomatoes next year.
5. refresh   Please refresh my memory as to why we are having a meeting today.
6. untwist   She will untwist the tie on the bread wrapper for them.
7. discuss   I would like to discuss the situation with you.
8. uncap   He did not want to uncap the new bottle of salad dressing.
9. unused   Please wrap up the unused portion for me to take home.
10. distaste   She had a distaste for sitting in traffic.
11. unsent   The unsent letter was in the drawer.
12. reface   We will reface the kitchen cabinets.
13. rerun   Ms. Jones will rerun the video for us.
14. reflex   When the nurse tapped her knee, her leg went up by reflex.
15. unmet   He was fired because of his many unmet deadlines.
16. never   I will never forget my trip to Hawaii.
17. distinct   That flower has a very distinct smell.
18. license   I need a special license to drive a truck.

Lesson 30–REVIEW LESSON

1. plenty   We have plenty of time to get home.
2. item   I only bought one item at the store.
3. puppet   The kids all enjoyed the lion puppet.
4. budget   We have to redo our yearly budget.
5. credit   I have one credit card in my wallet.
6. protect   You need to protect your bird from their cat.
7. second   I played second base at the game.
8. wages   Vince received his paycheck for the wages he had earned.
9. wisdom   Grandfather is full of wisdom.
10. adjust   Make sure you adjust your seatbelt to fit.
11. basic   The computer came with a free lesson to help me understand the basic functions.
12. sofa   Jill spilled soda on the sofa.
13. helmet   Make sure you wear a helmet every time you ride your bike.
14. cactus   The neighbor planted a large cactus in their front yard.
15. solid   The charm was made of solid gold.
16. any   Do you have any mittens I could borrow?
17. today   Today is the first day of summer.
18. never   Never walk into the street without looking for cars.

Lesson 31

1. involve   Don't involve Brian in the discussion.
2. impede   Talking to the T.V. reporters could impede the investigation.
3. immune   Gail thinks she is immune to the flu.
4. insult   Be careful not to insult the new neighbor.
5. import   The plan is to import the furniture from Asia.
6. infect   Be careful not to infect your sister with the flu.
7. impulse   His first impulse was to run when the dog chased him.
8. inept   Jill is totally inept at gardening.
9. improve   Jason plans to improve his grades next semester.
10. infest   Fleas could infest the carpet.
11. impress   Deliah tried to impress the principal with her knowledge.
12. intense   Studying for the entry exam was very intense.

13. impale   Joanne was glad she did not impale herself on the sharp piece of glass.

14. inspect   The fireman planned to inspect the classroom tomorrow.

15. imprint   The leaf left an imprint on the ground.

16. around   The store is around the corner.

17. aspirin   I took an aspirin for my headache.

18. interest   Becky's major interest is music.

Lesson 32

1. misuse   Be careful not to misuse the calling card your parents gave you.

2. mistake   I made one mistake on my test.

3. pretend   Adam likes to pretend to be a dinosaur.

4. mistrust   I do not mistrust my teacher.

5. prefer   I prefer to have Italian food for dinner.

6. misspell   How many words did you misspell?

7. prebake   You need to prebake the pie shell.

8. misdial   I will not misdial the number again.

9. mislead   Be careful not to mislead her into thinking she can come with us.

10. precut   Mr. Baxter told them to precut the yarn before art time.

11. prepaid   I have a prepaid calling card.

12. misprint   The joke in the newspaper contained one misprint.

13. preheat   Please preheat the oven to 350°.

14. misjudge   Do not misjudge her by looking at her appearance.

15. mismatch   Those socks are definitely a mismatch.

16. because   You are a true friend because you will always listen to me.

17. symbol   The symbol on his jacket stands for the school team.

18. thorough   Lisa was very thorough in planning the play.

Lesson 33

1. delete   I tried to delete the file.

2. defend   Ray had to defend himself when another student tried to start a fight.

3. preset   Preset the temperature to 65°.

4. defeat   The team was sure it would not face defeat.

5. deplete   Jasmine asked the girls not to deplete all the milk before breakfast.

6. delay   Do not delay in signing up for camp,

or you won't get in.

7. prerinse   Make sure you prerinse the vegetables before making a salad.

8. decline   Pam will decline the offer for the job.

9. deform   Rain may deform the clay statue.

10. preplan   She will preplan for college.

11. decode   It was hard to decode the secret message.

12. prevent   You need to stay inside today to prevent the spreading of your cold.

13. precede   Will John precede you to the platform?

14. prelaunch   Have they started the prelaunch sequence?

14. preflight   The pilot followed all the preflight directions.

16. again   Watch that car circle the block again.

17. bargain   I found a great bargain on the sale rack.

18. certain   Are you certain you passed the test?

Lesson 34

1. chalk   We wrote with chalk on the sidewalk.

2. walk   I will walk to the store at lunch.

3. wallet   I bought a red wallet today.

4. salt   Do you want salt on your potatoes?

5. wash   Did you wash your face yet?

6. watch   I forgot to wear my watch today.

7. talk   Jane likes to talk on the phone.

8. wander   The hiker did notwander off the path.

9. swap   Do you want to swap sandwiches?

10. halt   The policeman told us to halt when we tried to cross the street.

11. fall   Be careful no to fall into the creek.

12. walnut   Ben tried to crack the walnut open.

13. waltz   We want to learn how to waltz.

14. swamp   Frogs were croaking in the swamp.

15. stalk   We put a celery stalk in the soup.

16. through   The car went through the tunnel.

17. finally   I finally finished my homework!

18. favorite   My favorite food is chocolate.

Lesson 35

1. farmer   The farmer planted corn.

2. painter   I asked the painter to paint our room.

3. helper   Matthew was a great helper today!

4. actor   That actor is playing a new part.

5. planner   The wedding planner made sure the flowers were there on time.

6. catcher   I will play catcher in the next game.

7. doctor   I want to be a doctor when I grow up.

8. teacher   My mom is a teacher.
9. sailor   The sailor gets to come home soon.
10. dancer   Ray is a dancer in the play.
11. raptor   The raptor was a dangerous animal.
12. singer   Rebecca wants to be a singer.
13. driver   Our driver got us there on time.
14. captor   The captor was taken to jail.
15. traitor   There is a traitor among us.
16. together   Can we drive together?
17. surgeon   The surgeon performed three operations.
18. February   The second month of the year is February.

Lesson 36–REVIEW LESSON

1. improper   It was improper for you to ask for more food at dinner.
2. decrease   You need to decrease the amount of fat you are eating.
3. misprint   There was one misprint in the newspaper.
4. impose   I don't want to impose my ideas on you.
5. misfile   Make sure you don't misfile that folder.
6. impulse   My first impulse was to not eat at that restaurant.
7. defy   Don't defy your mother.
8. insane   Are you insane?
9. preserve   We want to preserve the oak trees.
10. injure   Don't injure yourself lifting those boxes.
11. misplace   Did you misplace the phone number?
12. instinct   The dog's instinct told him there was a cat nearby.
13. mistreat   Make sure you don't mistreat the cat.
14. defense   His defense was that he had an alibi.
15. prejudge   Do not prejudge Albert before the trial.
16. because   You need to rest because you have to get up early tomorrow.
17. through   I went through the garden gate.
18. together   We all went to the zoo together.

APPENDIX C

Name _____

Wheel of Spelling

HOW TO PLAY

1. Write, or have someone else write, your spelling words in the grid below.
2. List one or more spelling patterns chosen by your teacher on each pie piece below.
3. Attach a paperclip to serve as a spinner using a brad in the center of the circle as shown below.
4. Spin the paperclip each turn and use the spelling pattern to help create one of your spelling words on the numbered lines. Decide how many words you will spell.
5. If playing with a partner, the first person to create the right number of words, wins. If playing by yourself, set a challenge and see how many words you can create in a set amount of time.

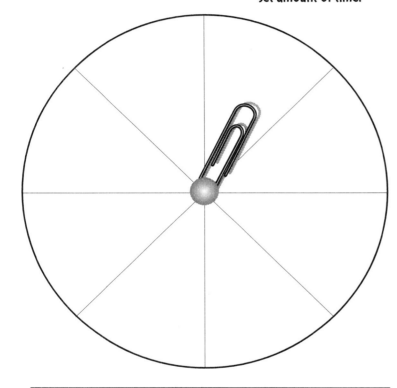

Spelling Words	

1. _____
2. _____
3. _____
4. _____
5. _____
6. _____
7. _____
8. _____
9. _____
10. _____

APPENDIX C

Spelling Gridlock

Name _____

How to Play
One person plays against another. Flip a coin to determine who plays first. The first player scores one point for putting down the first word. On each turn the player writes one of the spelling words for the week on the grid, placing one letter in each box going horizontally, vertically or diagonally. Words should not be written backwards! The goal is to score points by lining up words that have the same pattern of letters or by using a letter from another word as part of your new word. See examples below for the two ways to score points. After all the words in the list have been used, players may start over with the list again until all squares are filled. The player at at the end of the game with the most points wins.

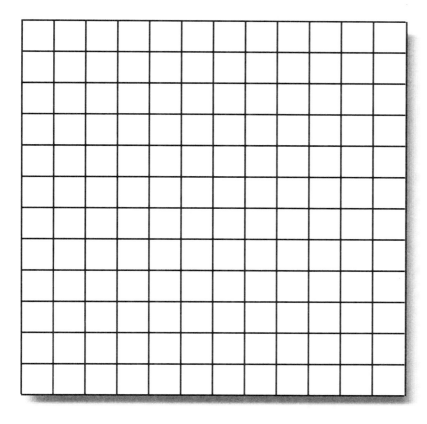

Scoring
The player who wrote *likely*, scored two points for lining up two letters with another word that matched.

The player who wrote *snowball*, scored four points for lining up four letters with another word that matched.
- **One point scored for each letter that matches!**

Points

Player 1	Player 2

173

Copyright © 2004 by High Noon Books. Permission granted to reproduce for classroom use.

Spelling Words from Words

Name _____

How to Play

Use your list of spelling words for the week. Write each spelling word on a separate piece of paper and place in container or paper bag to draw from. Draw one word at a time. Each time you draw a word, write it in the shaded box at the top of a column below. Use the letters from that word to make as many new words as you can. The new words can have fewer or the same numbers of letters as the word drawn.

Option: If playing against a friend, use a set amount of time (i.e. two minutes) and score a point for each new word made within the time limit. The player with the highest total of points for all rounds is the winner.

Write spelling words in the shaded box

1.	1.	1.	1.
2.	2.	2.	2.
3.	3.	3.	3.
4.	4.	4.	4.
5.	5.	5.	5.
6.	6.	6.	6.
7.	7.	7.	7.
8.	8.	8.	8.
9.	9.	9.	9.
10.	10.	10.	10.
11.	11.	11.	11.
12.	12.	12.	12.
13.	13.	13.	13.
14.	14.	14.	14.
15.	15.	15.	15.
Points - Round 1:	Points - Round 2:	Points - Round 3:	Points - Round 4:

Total Points

APPENDIX C
Spelling Baseball

Name _____

HOW TO PLAY

Play against a partner or team against team. If playing team against team, determine the batting order before play begins. On a separate piece of paper the teacher chooses and distributes to the pitcher a list of new and review spelling words. The words should be marked as singles, doubles, triples or home runs based on their spelling difficulty. A third person needs to be the pitcher and cannot play while the game is in progress. If playing in teams, one person on each team is designated a pitcher. Flip a coin to decide which team plays first. The batter for the team that's up requests a single double, triple, or home run word. If spelled correctly, the batter advances the correct number of bases and scores a run if home is reached. Batters continue to come up to bat until three outs are reached. A misspelled word determines an out. A game is complete after nine innings. To shorten the length of the game fewer innings can be played. Use coins to mark the runners on the game board below.

	1st Inning	2nd Inning	3rd Inning	4th Inning	5th Inning	6th Inning	7th Inning	8th Inning	9th Inning
TEAM 1									
TEAM 2									

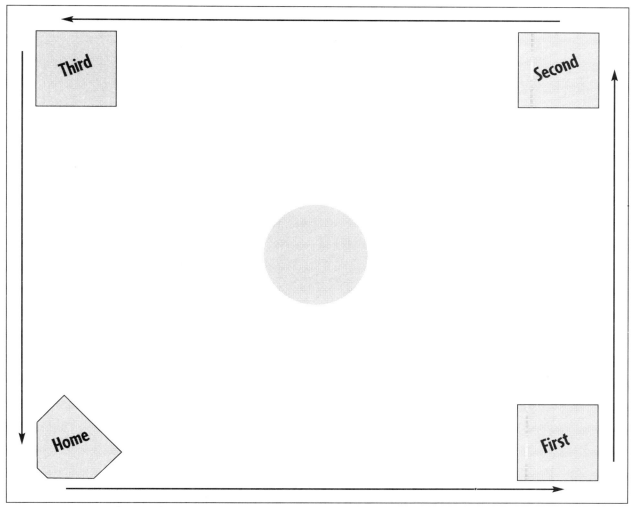